Daven *your* Age

An Adult Journey through the Daily Prayer Service

D0861429

*R*ABBI *Y*EHOSHUA *E*. *G*RUNSTEIN

gefen
publishing house   Est. 1981
JERUSALEM • NEW YORK

Cover Design: Benjie Herskowitz, Etc. Studios
Typesetting: Irit Nachum

ISBN: 978-965-229-599-6

1 3 5 7 9 8 6 4 2

Gefen Publishing House Ltd.
6 Hatzvi Street
Jerusalem 94386, Israel
972-2-538-0247
orders@gefenpublishing.com

Gefen Books
11 Edison Place
Springfield, NJ 07081
516-593-1234
orders@gefenpublishing.com

www.gefenpublishing.com

Printed in Israel

Send for our free catalog

Library of Congress Cataloging-in-Publication Data

Grunstein, Yehoshua, author.
Daven your age : an adult journey through the daily prayer service / Rabbi
Yehoshua Grunstein.
    pages cm
ISBN 978-965-229-599-6
1. Siddur.   2. Judaism—Liturgy.   3. Prayer—Judaism.   4. Amidah (Jewish
prayer) I. Title.
BM674.39G78 2013
296.4'5—dc23
                        2013024821

Contents

Part IV: The Amida: A Daily Audience with G-d | 115

Part V: From Daily Davening to Daily Life | 207

Acknowledgments

This work did not begin as a literary odyssey.

The crux of the style and ideas in these pages brings me back to the special four years I spent as the rabbi of the Beth Israel community of Halifax, Nova Scotia. As part of my duties, I was also the sole *baal tefilla* almost every day of the year. Going from a passive synagogue participant to a constant leader of the prayer service led me to raise many inquiries regarding what we should experience when opening the siddur each day of our lives. With the constant responsibility for guiding my congregants each day and week, and the ongoing difficulty maintaining a daily minyan, these ideas began to formulate. Moreover, it was at Beth Israel that I developed my speaking style, and it is to that community that I personally owe my own self-confidence to stand before a crowd and articulate ideas of possible interest. I therefore begin by thanking the wonderful Beth Israel family of Halifax, my home away from home, who led me to develop the seeds of these ideas. I am grateful to this community for what I received from them then, as well as for their continued and generous support and friendship now, far beyond the power that words on paper can express.

In this regard I recall, with great fondness and awe, the memory of the late Dr. Ralph Loebenberg, *z"l*, chief gabbai in Halifax during most of my tenure, in whose revered memory and tribute to his living legacy this book is dedicated and endowed by his beloved wife and growing progeny.

As the years went on, I noticed that the challenge of inspiring prayer is no different in Halifax than in most other locals in the world. Therefore, my first attempt to address it was during my triweekly class in the Zayit neighborhood of Efrat at the Singer Kollel, established in memory of Rabbi Pinchas Tzvi (Philip Singer), during the academic year of 5771. This book began as a series of lectures, under the heading "Why Don't You Pray Your Age?" to a group of devoted working men, whose schedule allowed them to spend their morning in setting a permanent time for learning Torah, while working in the late afternoon and evening. They were a continual sounding board for these ideas, and it is to them that I owe the systematic development of the ideas in these pages. Moreover, it is to them that I owe a year-long learning process and experience that was a true two-way street. I felt that through the year, I was praying differently and experiencing davening in a drastically different way, and thus it was a continual challenge for me to revisit what I had been doing since my first years of praying years before! Therefore, I want to express my gratitude to the Singer Kollel membership, not just for giving me the platform that obligated me to confront prayer at *this age*, but for being the sounding board as well, putting me through this experience, elevating my own level of prayer to higher realms, and allowing these ideas to move from the mind and heart to the oral word.

In this regard, I thank my parents, Tzvi and Tzippy Grunstein, for enabling me to study Torah for years at my alma mater, Yeshivat Har Etzion, where I was able devote my time solely to learning and self-development, under the leadership of its roshei yeshiva and outstanding staff. The privilege of spending many years in the rich vineyard of Torah continues to be appreciated greatly each time I have the self-discipline to learn and teach. Most specifically, it was there that the world of Halacha of prayer as well as the thought and lore of Rabbi J. B. Soloveitchik ("the Rav") were opened to me by his many students, whom I was privileged to have as my rabbeim and teachers – long before publications on this topic became widely available to the public. Much of this work is based on the insights and lessons I was taught in the Rav's name as I sat at their feet.

In addition, as this work goes to print, I deem it necessary, with much awe, to mention the deep and steadfast impact and lasting influence of my rebbe, Rav Yehuda Amital, *z"l*. The years I was privileged to see this giant "daven his age" before the Almighty as *chazan* on the High Holidays – each day, month, and year – stand before me as an elevated aspiration that I continue to strive toward as I serve as both a "davener" and a *baal tefilla* today. A glimpse of his many teachings and profound inspiration are quoted in this book, with the hope that I have accurately quoted his lasting wisdom, and with deep sorrow that he passed away before this could be presented to him.

As my lectures were recorded and uploaded to the YUTorah website (www.yutorah.org), they were heard by many that I have never met and some that I was privileged to actually meet. As a rather frequent traveler abroad to various Jewish communities and schools, I was privileged to hear many constructive comments on the lectures, which led me to consider transcribing and then editing the lectures into a book. As my travels are usually connected to visiting and servicing the many graduates of Ohr-Torah Stone's Straus-Beren Amiel Institute, where I am privileged to serve as director of training and placement, it was their consistent challenges of davening in their synagogues and schools around the globe that pushed me to move from the oral word to the written one. My thanks goes out to the entire staff of Straus-Beren Amiel and Ohr-Torah Stone, together with its many devoted emissaries in the field, for the motivation and for their encouragement to transform the ideas into a volume on the shelf.

With the devoted help, beyond the call of duty, of Tamar Ellis, who finished many an exhausting day of *sheirut leumi* (national service) in the very busy obstetrics ward of a Jerusalem hospital by listening to my NY-accented voice, the oral word developed into the written form, which was later edited into the book you see before you.

Rabbi David Singer, a dear neighbor and friend, and founder of the Singer Kollel mentioned above, encouraged the publication and first referred me to the devoted staff of Gefen Publishing House. It goes without saying that without the excitement and encouragement of Ilan Greenfield and Michael Fischberger for this project, the project coordinator Lynn Douek, together with the thorough and devoted editing work of Tziporah Levine, you would not be reading these lines. It's hard to put my gratitude into mere words when finally seeing this work in the form of a book due to their dedication and commitment.

My lectures on prayer at the Singer Kollel, and my attempt to transfer it to the written word, would not have happened if not for my dear wife, Tali, ensuring that all our kids were out on time in the morning so I could teach my classes, as well as generously giving me the time to work on the manuscript for many long evenings. While being a mother to Noam, Aviva, Amichai, and Ayelet, intertwined with functioning as a full-time lawyer, she was part and parcel of the rigorous editing process and specifically rereading the entire book, adding insights to the style and ideas, all the while taking full charge of our home. The great tannaitic sage, Rabbi Akiva, was absent for so many years from home fully engrossed in Torah study, only to return home and firmly say about his wife Rachel שלי ושלכם שלה הוא, "What is mine and what is yours belong to her" (Ketuvot 63a). If Rabbi Akiva could say that after being away from his wife during all the years of his learning, how much more so in my case. Tali was part of this written work directly and up close, and I truthfully state, with love and admiration, this work is yours as much as mine.

Finally, I stand before the Almighty G-d in awe and thanks, for allowing me the privilege to labor in the rich vineyard He gave the Jewish people, and to teach the profound and everlasting beauty of His Torah to His people.

Introduction: Daven Your Age

The amount of time we pray per year is enormous! We stand to daven each day for about an hour (divided into three times a day). Factoring in the longer Shabbat and holiday prayers and Musaf, multiplied by 365 days a year, we end up spending five hundred hours per year standing before the Almighty in prayer![1] Multiplying that by the amount of years we live, we are speaking of hundreds of days.

One would think that with this vast investment of time spent in prayer, we would be experts in the field.

But has anything changed since our prayer experience in grade school? Have we been challenged further in the realm of davening? With our sages dictating so much time per year devoted to prayer, isn't it uncanny to realize that we seem to be static in our development in the prayer service?

While one can complete more books of the Bible each year, explore and comprehend additional tractates of the Talmud, and increase one's proficiency in Jewish law and thought, it seems that one area will inevitably remain the same: prayer!

When was the last time you learned about praying? Most of us stop learning about prayer by seventh grade, when we were

---

[1] I thank my colleague, Rabbi Betzalel Safra, for this statistic.

taught the final renditions of the siddur. Since then, was there ever an avenue to enhance your praying?

In contradistinction, I am sure that your proficiency in the world of Jewish law and lore, and even in the actual laws of prayer, has surely developed from the first time you were exposed to it till the time you read these lines. Beyond quantitatively gaining more knowledge, a discussion on a law of Shabbat, the weekly parsha, a contemporary Jewish issue, or even an interesting question relating to the laws or customs of prayer will surely be suited to the age and intellectual capability of the people involved in the discussion, and will be viewed on a vastly different level than when these same issues were first introduced in grade school.

And yet, most Jews, in any Jewish educational system, have not been taught that much about the experience of prayer since childhood!

Even with the large amount of literature available,[2] with endless translations on the contemporary siddur and beyond, I don't believe that we were educated, nor overly encouraged, to invest time and effort in this realm. We tend to think that this area of study has long been exhausted, together with learning how to wash our hands and keep our clothing clean! As a typical graduate of the Orthodox Jewish educational system, I have heard teachers endlessly encourage their students to develop in Torah learning and in keeping its mitzvot. But while my memory is far from being totally firm, I don't recall the command to *develop your prayer….*

Thus, there is a clear and present danger that each time the siddur is opened, we are coming before G-d and *praying like we did in grade school, and we thus emerge from davening with a primitive experience in hand!*

---

[2] Twenty thousand results on the topic come up when the phrase "books on Jewish prayer" is put in Google.

We were all taught to be age appropriate in other realms ("pick on someone your own size"), yet we come to one of the most frequent and sacred ventures in our life and approach it like kids!

- Our Modeh Ani takes on the significance that our preschool teacher taught.
- Our Birkot Hashachar are said with the *kavana* taught in first grade.
- Our Amida before G-d is at about the level of fourth grade.

It is therefore no surprise that Rabbi Donin can assert that "We live in an age when it is not fashionable to pray."[3] Fashion is a result of the subjective environment in which one functions, and when prayer remains at a far lower level than where one is today, it's no surprise that it's not in "fashion." Moreover, the Rav asserted, rather naturally, that "many a Jew does not like to daven, but would love to have davened!"[4]

The words of the Rav reverberate in my mind as I write these pages. The issue detailed above is an age-old problem, and this book is not intended to reinvent the wheel. Nor is it an attempt to speak about prayer in the abstract, as many others have already done. Rather, this book is specifically tailored to bridge one particular "gap" that I believe we all possess – between the laws of prayer and the experience of prayer.[5] Utilizing the Rav's distinction above, I hope that the joy one feels when he has "davened" will at

---

[3] Rabbi Hayim Halevy Donin, *To Pray As A Jew: A Guide to the Prayer Book and the Synagogue Service* (Basic Books, 1991), page 4.

[4] Said to me by my rebbe and rosh yeshiva, Rabbi Aharon Lichtenstein שליט״א, in July of 1999, when I became the gabbai (in charge of the regular facilitation of davening) at Yeshivat Har Etzion.

[5] I am far from being the first to try and bridge this gap, and I believe the gap still exists. See the grand vision of Rav A. Y. Hakohen Kook, *Orot Hakodesh* 1, *shaar* 1, *seder* 2:18, as well as *Orot Hatorah* 13:4:6.

least be equal, if not far more substantial, for the person who has genuinely prayed.

It's hard to comprehend a situation in which we seem to develop in every other area *surrounding prayer* – with advanced lectures on the times of prayer, the place to pray, the laws governing it, and mistakes that can result – and yet the very act itself, performed more than any other daily Jewish activity, is experienced in the very same way we experienced it so many years before.

I fear that there is a real disconnect between people's knowledge of prayer and their experience of prayer. I fear that many an adult Jew, sophisticated and educated in so many realms of Judaism, might be having a prayer experience far beneath his or her "size" or age, *without connecting prayer to his or her knowledge about prayer*. As I travel around the world, I've met hundreds of Jews, of varying levels of observance, who know when to stand, sit, and even know when to kiss their tefillin during the service, and yet have no idea *how that impacts what they say and feel*. As Simon Wolf commented strongly:

> When a child looks at his parent, he sees an educated, well-accomplished professional – an adult but an adult practicing his Judaism like an eighteen-year-old (or maybe someone even younger).… He easily discerns the sophistication with which his parents approach the planning of a simchah, the building of a house, their social interactions and work, a sophistication that is absent in the religious realm of their lives. A child is acutely aware that his parents know more about the features of their smartphone or car than they do about their tefillin, Shabbat and yom tov observance, and the weekly parashah.… There is only one solution to this problem: Parents have to apply the same sophistication, tenacity, maturity and commitment to their religious practice as they do to other aspects of their lives. Learn Torah like an adult.

> Pray like an adult. Do chesed like an adult. In short,
> practice religion like the adult one has become.[6]

As my esteemed neighbor, Professor Jeffery Wolf, once wittily commented, "I read an entire book regarding the laws of prayer, and I can promise you – *davening wasn't in there!*"

The practical ramifications of our predicament are many. For an example, it's never been a wonder to me that the level of talking and noise in our contemporary shul is high.[7] Despite the many laws forbidding talking at various junctures of the service,[8] conversations still persist.

This same talking seldom happens during a sermon or lecture, or during a wedding ceremony or eulogy, even if they are as long as the prayer service that day. It seems to me that the reason for this distinction is rather obvious: while we listen and hopefully internalize sermons as adults, we're still praying as children!

This is a built-in problem when one is strict about his observance of the laws of the Torah, and yet doesn't relate to the spiritual aspect of these laws. And yet, in the "work of the heart" of prayer, this can at times be critically damaging as we pray no less than three times daily, and it can turn into a mundane task rather than a lofty spiritual experience. In the words of the late Talner Rebbe, Rabbi Professor Isadore Twersky, *z"l*:

> A tense dialectical relationship between religion in
> essence and religion in manifestation is at the core
> of the Jewish religious consciousness.... Halakhah
> is the indispensable manifestation and prescribed
> concretization of an underlying and overriding

---

[6] Letter to the editor, *Jewish Action*, Spring 5772/April 2012, page 4. Reprinted with permission of Mr. Wolf.

[7] This phenomenon has many other explanations that are beyond the scope of this work, but I believe the above is one of the central ones.

[8] See, for example, *Code of Jewish Law*, OC 54:4, 57:2, 88:1, 125:2, 131:1.

spiritual essence.... The tension flows from the
painful awareness that manifestation and essence
sometimes drift apart, from the sober recognition that
a carefully constructed, finely chiseled normative
system cannot regularly reflect or energize interior,
fluid spiritual forces and motives. Yet, if the system is
to remain vibrant, it must.[9]

I believe this problem can be addressed and mitigated. In a phrase
coined above by Rabbi Twersky, I would argue that our prayer
service will change if we can connect "religion in essence and
religion in manifestation." If we are able *to connect between
our knowledge of laws of prayer and our experience of prayer*,
I believe that they can be linked. As we hold the siddur in our
hands, we can merge our already existing knowledge about the
laws of prayer with prayer itself. Hopefully, by combining them,
the latter will be brought up to the level of the former, and we may
perhaps be privileged to enjoy an adult experience of prayer.

Therefore, the goal of these pages is to attempt to bring the level
of prayer up to the level of our knowledge of the laws governing
it, and allow the very laws of prayer to influence its experience.

I believe our personal service, our minyan, and the environment
in our community synagogues and school synagogues will change
drastically if our efforts succeed. At the very least, I hope these
pages will result in a substantial stride in that direction.

As you read through these pages you will not find a
comprehensive interpretation of every prayer in the siddur. Nor
will you see any notes on variation of customs as to what is said

---

[9] Isador Twersky, "Religion and Law," in *Religion in a Religious Age*, ed. S.
D. Goitein (Cambridge, MA: Association for Jewish Studies, 1974). I thank
my revered teacher, Rabbi Jacob J. Schacter (whom I was privileged to meet
for the first time through Ralph Loebenberg, *z"l*, who encouraged me to join
one of Rabbi Schacter's many seminars for rabbis), for referring me to this
source many times over the years.

daily and what is not. Rather, you will see an attempt to take a Jew's knowledge of the laws of prayer and transform them into an experience of praying, any day of the year.[10]

Moreover, you will find that the language is often in the second person, as it's my hope that this can serve as a tool for the realistic prayer experience.

For those who would like to use this book as an ongoing guide, a section at the end of the book summarizes the main themes and can be quickly glanced at either daily or weekly. While each chapter tries to elaborate on the topic, the small summary at its end attempts to give over the concise idea expressed in each chapter.

Recently, I attended a local Purim *shpiel* (party) that dealt with the challenge of cutting onions on the eve of Shabbat, without having the scent on one's hands for the entirety of the holy day. In this regard, it's my hope and genuine prayer that this book will enable our davening to create a lasting scent, and that the scent of prayer should stay on our bodies and souls. My sincere hope, in bringing this work before the davener, is to see the plea of David Hamelech (King David), said each day in our own davening in u'Va l'Tzion, come to fruition as we stand before G-d in prayer:

ה' אלוקי אברהם יצחק וישראל אבותינו, שמרה זאת לעולם **ליצר מחשבות לבב עמך** והכן לבבם **אליך.** (דברי הימים א, כט:יח)

> G-d of Avraham, Yitzchak, and Yaakov, keep this forever, the impulse of *the thoughts of the hearts of Your people*, and direct their hearts *to You*. (I Divrei Hayamim 29:18)

---

[10] For organizational purposes, while lectures and material were delivered concerning the prayer services on Shabbat, the holidays, and other special days of the year, this book will concentrate on the weekly service, much of which can be applied to the special days as well. G-d willing, I hope that more material specific to these days will also become available in written form as we head further into the second decade of the twenty-first century.

רבא חזייה לרב המנונא דקא מאריך בצלותיה, אמר: מניחין חיי עולם ועוסקים בחיי שעה! והוא סבר: זמן תפלה לחוד, וזמן תורה לחוד.

רבי ירמיה הוה יתיב קמיה דרבי זירא, והוו עסקי בשמעתא. נגה לצלויי, והוה קא מסרהב רבי ירמיה, קרי עליה רבי זירא: (משלי כח:ט) "מסיר אזנו משמע תורה גם תפלתו תועבה" (תלמוד בבלי, מסכת שבת דף י עמוד א)

Raba was watching R. Hamnuna, who was extending the duration of his prayers for a very long time. He said [to him], "You forsake eternal life [i.e., the study of Torah] and devote yourself to temporary life [i.e., prayer]!" But he [R. Hamnuna] held, "The times for prayer and for [the study of] Torah are distinct from one another."

R. Yirmiya was sitting before R. Zeira engaged in study. As it was growing very late for them to pray on time, R. Yirmiya was making signs to R. Zeira to adjourn the class. Thereupon R. Zeira applied to him [the following verse], "He who has turned away from hearing the law, even his prayer is an abomination" (Mishlei 28:9). (Shabbat 10a)

Often quoted by my rebbe, Rav Yehuda Amital, *z"l*

ר' נחמן ביקש להפוך את התורות שלו לתפילות, ואכן תלמידו ר' נתן מילא את בקשתו בעשרות תורות שהפך אותן לתפילות. דומה שהגיע הזמן לחשוב איך להפוך את התפילות – לתורות.

R. Nachman [from Braslav] wanted to transform his Torah into prayers. And indeed, his student R. Natan fulfilled his wish with the tens of words of Torah that were changed into prayers. It seems that it's time to change the prayers into words of Torah.

Rav Yehuda Amital, *z"l*

Part I

A Jew at Prayer

Pouring Our Hearts Out to G-d…Today?

Let's be honest – davening daily is an annoyance!

Not only must we pray every day, we are commanded to pray the same words, three times a day! To add salt to our wounds, these prayers are supposed to take place outside the comfortable confines of our home, be it at the synagogue or at one of the "spontaneous" minyanim organized "on the run." Even a newcomer to Judaism, with the strongest motivation and excitement for their newly acquired Jewish lifestyle, would surely find davening...an annoyance!

And yet, when the Gemara looks for a source for prayer, it defines prayer as the work of the heart:

> דתניא "לאהבה את ה' אלהיכם ולעבדו בכל לבבכם" (דברים יא:יד)
> – איזו היא עבודה שהיא בלב? הוי אומר, זו תפלה. (תענית ב.)

> A tannaitic source taught: "And you shall love the Lord your G-d, and serve Him *with all your heart*" (Devarim 11:14) – what is the service that is in *one's heart*? This is prayer. (Taanit 2a)

This wasn't always the case. There was a time when *tefilla* (prayer) was a spontaneous, emotional experience "of the heart." Thus, the Talmud states:

רבי יוסי ברבי חנינא אמר: **תפלות אבות תקנום**... תניא כוותיה דרבי
יוסי ברבי חנינא:
אברהם תקן תפלת שחרית, שנאמר "וישכם אברהם בבקר אל
המקום אשר **עמד** שם" (בראשית יט:כז), ואין עמידה אלא תפלה...
יצחק תקן תפלת מנחה, שנאמר "ויצא יצחק לשוח בשדה
לפנות ערב" (בראשית כד:סג), ואין שיחה אלא תפלה...
יעקב תקן תפלת ערבית, שנאמר "ויפגע במקום וילן שם"
(בראשית כח:יא), ואין פגיעה אלא תפלה... (ברכות כו:)

R. Yossi ben R. Chanina says: *Prayer was instituted by
our forefathers*.... A tannaitic source [i.e., a *beraita*]
supports the view of R. Yossi ben R. Chanina:

Avraham instituted the Shacharit [morning] prayer,
as it states, "Avraham got up early in the morning, to
the place where he had *stood*" (Bereishit 19:27) – and
"standing" means praying....

Yitzchak instituted the Mincha [afternoon] prayer,
as it says, "Yitzchak went to *speak* in the field toward
evening" (Bereishit 24:63) – and "speaking" means
praying....

Yaakov instituted the Maariv [evening] prayer,
as it says, "He *hit upon* that place and lay down
there" (Bereishit 28:11) – and "hit" means prayer....
(Berachot 26b)

Let's picture the scenes the Talmud beautifully describes:

- Avraham returns bright and early to the very place where he
  had pleaded for the salvation of the cities of Sedom and Amora
  the day before. This was not a planned service, with set text
  and tunes! Rather, it was a spontaneous plea to G-d, as a direct
  result of hearing about G-d's plan to destroy these cities.

- Yitzchak walking out of his home toward evening, as the day
  is about to transform (both literally and figuratively) from light
  to darkness, to spontaneously seek a connection with G-d in
  these last moments of light.

- Yaakov is running for his life from his bloodthirsty brother Esav, who desires his younger brother's death. Yaakov seeks refuge in the home of his maternal grandfather, whom he has never met. This clear and present feeling of danger for his very life, intertwined with the vulnerable feeling of moving toward the unknown, motivates Yaakov to seek out G-d's salvation in the darkness.

Our forefathers' experiences are a far cry from mandated, regulated prayer. Quite the contrary – they are unstructured, perhaps impulsive expressions during moments of need. Indeed, the Gemara above refers to the act of praying as *avoda shehi balev*, service of/in the *heart*. In looking for a source for the mitzva to open your heart before G-d, it's no wonder that the Gemara points to these three cases of "hearts opening" to G-d – be it in moments of distress (Avraham), elevation (Yitzchak), or danger (Yaakov).

Countless other examples throughout the Bible correspond to this "spur-of-the-moment," heartfelt prayer. To quote but a few:

- Paroh is struck with a plague of hail, and beseeches Moshe to plead with G-d that the plague be brought to an immediate halt.[1]

- Miriam, Moshe's sister, is punished with *tzaraat* and Moshe turns to G-d to heal her. Her illness engenders a spontaneous expression of prayer from her brother, with just five words: "And Moshe called out to G-d, saying, 'My G-d, please heal her!'"[2]

- The Jewish people have just sinned against the Land of Israel, believing in the slanderous report of the spies who had been sent to scout the land. G-d, so to speak, "had enough" (as this was far from the first sin), and declared the intention to destroy

---

[1] Shemot 9:27–29.
[2] Bamidbar 12:10–13.

the Jewish people. In this cardinal hour of the need of physical survival from this Divine decree, Moshe bursts forth in prayer to attempt to save the Jewish people from total annihilation.[3]

- Moshe requests to enter the Holy Land, following G-d's decree to the contrary.[4]

- After enduring years of infertility, and her counterpart Penina's barbs, Chana stands before G-d in the Tabernacle and prays.[5]

- Yona pleads for his life from the midst of the whale that had swallowed him alive.[6]

- King Chizkiyahu beseeches G-d to remove the forces of King Sancheriv surrounding him,[7] and asks G-d to heal him from an (assumed) terminal sickness.[8]

But we don't have to look only to the past. Think of yourself today – be it when someone close to you was ill, or when you prayed for the first time at the Kotel, I am sure that your communication with G-d was a spontaneous and heartfelt prayer.

Attentive to the Torah's view of prayer, and the aforementioned Talmudic statement, the Rambam codifies the biblical commandment to pray as follows:

מצות עשה להתפלל בכל יום, שנאמר, "ועבדתם את ה' אלקיכם". מפי השמועה למדו שעבודה זו היא תפלה, שנאמר, "ולעבדו בכל לבבכם". אמרו חכמים: אי זו היא עבודה שבלב? זו תפלה". **ואין מנין התפלות מן התורה, ואין משנה התפלה הזאת מן התורה, ואין לתפלה זמן קבוע מן התורה.** (משנה תורה, הלכות תפילה ונשיאת כפיים א:א)

---

[3] Ibid. 14:11–20.
[4] Devarim 3:23–25.
[5] I Shmuel 1:10–13.
[6] Yona 2:2–11.
[7] II Melachim 19:10–36.
[8] Ibid. 20:1–6.

There is a positive commandment to pray each day, as it says, "And you shall serve the Lord your G-d"; our tradition teaches that "service" is prayer, as it says, "And you shall serve [G-d] with all your heart." State our sages: "What is the service of the heart? It is prayer." And *neither the number of prayers, nor their text, nor their times are established by the Bible.* (*Mishneh Torah, Hilchot Tefilla u'Nesiat Kapayim* 1:1)

No set time, no set text, just an opening of the heart before G-d when needed.

The Ramban goes even further. Disagreeing with the Rambam, he claims that there is absolutely *no obligation* to pray – except in times of danger or need:

ודאי כל ענין התפלה **אינו חובה כלל**, אבל הוא ממדות חסד הבורא
יתברך עלינו ששומע ועונה בכל קראינו אליו... וזה כענין שכתוב
"וכי תבאו מלחמה בארצכם על הצר הצורר אתכם והרעותם
בחצוצרות ונזכרתם לפני ה' אלקיכם" (במדבר י:ט). והיא מצוה
על כל צרה וצרה שתבא על הצבור לצעוק לפניו בתפלה ובתרועה.
(השגות הרמב"ן על הרמב"ם, ספר המצוות, מצוות עשה ה)

Prayer is *not an obligation at all*, but rather derives from G-d's kindness to us in listening and responding each time we call out to G-d…. As it states, "If you enter into battle in your land against an enemy who is oppressing you, you shall blow the trumpets and be remembered before the Lord your G-d" (Bamidbar 10:9). This is a commandment to beseech G-d with prayer and trumpets whenever any danger comes upon the community. (Ramban's glosses on the Rambam's *Sefer Hamitzvot*, positive commandment no. 5)

Thus, according to the view of the Ramban, prayer *can't* be a daily mitzva due to *its spontaneous nature of genuinely opening one's heart* that is contrary to any form or structure. Rather, communication with G-d must come as an emotional response to a threatening reality. When we don't feel the need, we are not obligated to pray, because such prayers wouldn't constitute "the service of the heart."

But returning to the Gemara, we find that there is yet another source for prayer:

רבי יהושע בן לוי אמר: תפלות כנגד תמידין תקנום... ותניא כוותיה
דרבי יהושע בן לוי:

מפני מה אמרו תפלת השחר עד חצות? שהרי תמיד של שחר
קרב והולך עד חצות. ורבי יהודה אומר: עד ארבע שעות, שהרי
תמיד של שחר קרב והולך עד ארבע שעות.

ומפני מה אמרו תפלת המנחה עד הערב? שהרי תמיד של בין
הערבים קרב והולך עד הערב. רבי יהודה אומר: עד פלג המנחה,
שהרי תמיד של בין הערבים קרב והולך עד פלג המנחה.

ומפני מה אמרו תפלת הערב אין לה קבע? שהרי אברים ופדרים
שלא נתעכלו מבערב קרבים והולכים כל הלילה.

ומפני מה אמרו של מוספין כל היום? שהרי קרבן של מוספין
קרב כל היום. רבי יהודה אומר: עד שבע שעות, שהרי קרבן מוסף
קרב והולך עד שבע שעות. (ברכות כו:)

R. Yehoshua ben Levi said: Prayer was instituted to correspond to the daily *tamid* sacrifices brought in the Temple.... And indeed a *beraita* affirms the position of R. Yehoshua ben Levi:

Why do the sages say that the prayer of the morning is until midday? Since the *tamid* sacrifice of the morning was sacrificed till midday.

And why did they say that the Mincha service is until evening? Since the *tamid* sacrifice of the afternoon was sacrificed till evening. R. Yehuda said:

Till *plag hamincha*,[9] since the *tamid* of the afternoon
would be sacrificed till *plag hamincha*.

And why did they say that the evening prayer has
no end time? Since the various parts of the sacrifices
that were not consumed during the previous day can
be consumed [on the Altar] all night.

And why did they say that the Musaf prayer is all
day? Since the Musaf sacrifice can be brought all day.
R. Yehuda says: Only for the [first] seven hours of the
day, since the Musaf sacrifice was brought only during
the [first] seven hours of the day. (Berachot 26b)

Instead of instinctive, unstructured prayer, the above passage in
the Gemara provides exact times to pray, every day, just like the
sacrifices were offered on the Altar daily.

Transforming outpourings of the heart into predetermined
prayer is a *huge* change! The Rambam explains this revolution
and establishes the new rules regarding prayer today:

כיון שגלו ישראל בימי נבוכדנצר הרשע נתערבו בפרס ויון ושאר
האומות...ואינם מכירים לדבר יהודית... ומפני זה כשהיה אחד
מהן מתפלל תקצר לשונו לשאול חפציו, או להגיד שבח הקדוש
ברוך הוא בלשון הקדש... וכיון שראה עזרא ובית דינו כך עמדו
ותקנו להם שמנה עשרה ברכות על הסדר; שלש ראשונות שבח
לה' ושלש אחרונות הודיה, ואמצעיות יש בהן שאלת כל הדברים
שהן כמו אבות לכל חפצי איש ואיש ולצרכי הציבור כולן... ומפני
ענין זה תקנו כל הברכות והתפלות מסודרות בפי כל ישראל כדי
שיהא ענין כל ברכה ערוך בפי העלג. וכן תקנו שיהא מנין התפלות
כמנין הקרבנות... נמצאו התפלות בכל יום שלש, ערבית ושחרית

9　About an hour and a quarter before the end of the "day." The Gemara is
speaking about *shaot zemaniyot* – halachic divisions of time that are
calculated by dividing into twelve the amount of time between sunrise and
sunset, or dawn to dusk, on a given day. Though referred to as "hours," these
do not correspond to sixty-minute units.

ומנחה, ובשבתות ובמועדים ובראשי חדשים ארבע, שלש של כל
יום ותפלת המוספין... (לעיל, הלכה ד)

Since the Jewish people were exiled in the times of
Nevuchadnetzar and they assimilated into Persia,
Greece, and other nations…and they didn't know
how to speak Hebrew…. And therefore, when one of
them prayed, they didn't have the ability to verbally
express petition or to offer praise to G-d in Hebrew….
When Ezra and his court saw this, *they established
eighteen blessings in order.* The first three are praise,
the last three are thanksgiving, and the middle ones
are all petitions, which are like chapter headings for
all the needs of the individual and the community
as a whole…. And therefore they established all the
blessings and prayers on the lips of all Israel, so that
each blessing could be said by even the ignorant. And
they also established that the number of the prayers
would parallel the number of sacrifices…. Thus we see
three prayers daily: Maariv, Shacharit, and Mincha.
And on Shabbat and holidays there would be four
– the daily three and the Musaf prayer…. (*Mishneh
Torah, Hilchot Tefilla u'Nesiat Kapayim* 1:4)

From the heartfelt experience of standing before G-d in a time of
genuine need, we move to a daily obligation to recite the same
basic prayer every day, three times a day. As the Gemara concisely
concludes:

אמר לך רבי יוסי ברבי חנינא: לעולם אימא לך תפלות אבות
תקנום, **ואסמכינהו רבנן אקרבנות.** (ברכות כו:)

Says R. Yossi ben R. Chanina: Indeed, it is well
established that the forefathers ordained prayer, *but
the rabbis anchored them to the sacrifices.* (Berachot
26b)

Our sages took the innovative, spontaneous concept of prayer initiated by our forefathers, but added the parallel to the sacrifices, mandating that prayer occur every day, just like the daily sacrifices. Our sages thus codified davening as a consistent obligation thrice daily, preferably in a specific location and with a specific text.

The establishment of formal prayer directly impinges upon the concept of *avoda she'balev*, "service of the *heart*," which the Rambam above understands to be the essence of prayer! How can the "service of the heart" take a direct hit, and be replaced with a daily obligation to pray, whether our heart is in it or not?

Unlike spontaneous prayer, the established text is the same every day, it's in a foreign language, and it may not be recited at your preferred pace when praying with others in a minyan. As I heard from a colleague returning from a convention of rabbis discussing the state of contemporary prayer in their synagogues: "We are asking Jews to pray in a language they don't know, in a place they don't want to be, for things they don't really need!" Basically, even a trained monkey could daven from the regulated prayer book, with tefillin on his arm and head! What would be the difference between the Jew and the monkey, in terms of their experience, if neither feels the need to speak to G-d?

Let's face it – we are not emotionally elevated every day. On the contrary, we're often annoyed three times a day! While the morning Shacharit service may technically be a bit easier, as it becomes part of our morning routine, inserting Mincha and Maariv into our daily schedule can be aggravating – and the added expectation of heartfelt prayer under such circumstances can be quite tiresome. Take the following familiar scenarios:

- It's 4:00 p.m. in the winter, sunset is looming at 4:40 p.m., and you're in the middle of a conference call. You could finish the call within the hour and be on your way home by 5:00 – but alas, not you. You have to leave it all and try to find a minyan, further prolonging your day.

- You finally reach home at 8:00 pm. Your head hurts and your throat is sore, and all you'd like to do is eat dinner and relax before retiring. But *no* – the shoes can't come off yet, since you still have to daven Maariv.

- And then, you're on "vacation." The kids are enjoying the water park, and you're enjoying their smiles. But your watch says that there are just ten minutes left till the cutoff time for Mincha…so you have to stop it all and find a corner to pray, with the *kvetches* of "Why did we have to get out of the pool?" as background music!

Despite all the above being true, I contend that Chazal (our sages) were amazingly insightful in establishing these prayers. While the demands of set prayer can be quite annoying, the results of this system are critical to us. Allow me to introduce this idea with an analogy from another "annoyance" in our life: commercials.

As you know, a good commercial is one that is not shown all at once, but rather at different intervals of seconds during a given hour of a TV show. As the company pays quite a lot for units of airtime, why not devote one whole minute to their product? Why do we keep hearing about the product for twenty-second intervals throughout the show?

Annoying? Yes. But since you hear about the product throughout the show, the chance that the jingle will stay firmly in your heads is much greater than if you had watched it only once.

Actually, the advertising experts didn't get the idea from thin air; the source of the term "service of the heart" comes from the very book in the Bible where this system is tried…by Moshe himself. The book of Devarim makes any rabbi look good – no matter how long the speech, it will seem short compared to that of Moshe Rabbeinu. He opens his mouth at the beginning of the book of Devarim, and closes his mouth toward the end of the very last parsha. And in this very long speech, constituting almost the entirety of this fifth book of the Bible, he repeats concepts over and over again.[10]

Why didn't Moshe just say things once? We would have heard, understood, and moved on to the next theme.

The answer suggested by Bible teacher David Nativ is that Moshe knew exactly what our sages later understood, and advertisement agencies have now learned: in order for a message to penetrate, *it has to be repeated over and over and over again at different times and intervals*. Moshe didn't make his speech all in one day; he went on for several months, and each time he repeated the most vital themes. By doing this, the themes of the speech did not only create a cognitive awareness of their importance; after hearing them repeatedly, these themes hopefully also penetrated the minds and souls of the people.

Praying three times a day gives us consistent spiritual reminders, every single day! Thrice a day, your religion, the core of who you are – far more than your position at the office or in the community – is inserted into your life whether you want it or not, just like that commercial jingle. Be it at work or in the comfort of your home, every few hours you are reminded of your Jewishness.

If not for mandated prayer, we could go through an entire day without focusing on the core beliefs of our very essence as Jews, expressed in the text of the daily service.

This is true on two levels: the personal, and what should be the personal.

On the personal level, things change in your life, moods shift in your daily routine, decisions need to be made...and with all this happening, when is there time to connect any of this with

---

[10] The command to love G-d, for example, appears in Devarim 10:12; 11:13, 22; 19:9; 30:6, 16; and 30:20, and the directive to serve G-d with all our hearts and souls appears in Devarim 4:29; 6:5; 10:12; 26:16; and 30:2, 6, 10.

your religion and your fundamental values? The sages of the Talmud Yerushalmi said it best:

מאיכן למדו שלש תפילות? ר' שמואל בר נחמני אמר: כנגד ג'
פעמים שהיום משתנה על הבריות.
בשחר צריך אדם לומר: "מודה אני לפניך ה' אלקי ואלקי אבותי
שהוצאתני מאפילה לאורה".
במנחה צריך אדם לומר: "מודה אני לפניך ה' אלקי ואלקי אבותי,
כשם שזכיתני לראות החמה במזרח כך זכיתי לראות במערב".
בערב צריך לומר: "יהי רצון מלפניך, ה' אלקי ואלקי אבותי,
כשם שהייתי באפילה והוצאתני לאורה כך תוציאני מאפילה
לאורה". (ירושלמי, ברכות ד:א)

From where did they learn [to pray] three times? R. Shmuel ben Nachmani said: From the three times daily that the day changes upon the creatures.

In the morning, one must say: "I thank you, my G-d and the G-d of my forefathers, for taking me out from darkness to light."

In the afternoon, one must say: "I thank you, my G-d and the G-d of my forefathers, just as You have privileged me to see the sun in the east, so may You privilege me to see the sun in the west."

In the evening, one must say: "May it be Your will, my G-d and the G-d of my forefathers, that just as I was in darkness and You took me out to light, so may You take me out from darkness to light." (Yerushalmi, Berachot 4:1)

The day changes, and your needs change accordingly. In the morning, you have a full day ahead of you in which you can be creative and productive. The sunshine gives you hope, happiness, and motivation to tackle yet another day. In the middle of the day, so much is happening in your life – work, meetings, errands.

Your goal is to "see the sun in the west" – may this day end well, allowing me to overcome the many challenges that I'm in the midst of right now. In the evening, with darkness all around you, the fear of wasting precious time, and the feelings of helplessness that darkness evokes, are now running through your head. Therefore your plea to G-d is to yet see "the light" – to see another day in which you can accomplish more.

These transitions can't be void of G-d and Judaism. Thus, the sages ordained that at these three daily points, you stand before G-d – with whatever you genuinely feel at that moment, connecting the two.

Aside from prayer, how does your Judaism actually express itself? After all, we do what all members of the human race do: we get up, keep healthy, work for a living, raise children, nurture our relationships with our loved ones, and enjoy life. How is any of this related to your religion?

Established prayer bridges the gap between your religion and your day. It creates opportunities to talk to G-d about your life.

But this idea goes much further than your own life and religious stance. Even if you do connect your personal needs with G-d, days can go by without you ever having a care about the world around you. The Amida's "thirteen blessings of petition," its middle and core, prevent that from occurring. These thirteen *berachot* speak about the world's many needs, including health, making a proper living, rain, restoring a moral justice system, together with the need for full redemption. People who do not make davening a part of their day can go through an entire day, never giving a second thought to the acute needs of others. They make their own money and take care of their own families, but they are insensitive to the community and world around them. True, they may listen to the radio, read the morning papers, and pay close attention to the news each night. But how many actually do something about it? How many speak to someone to rectify the world's many problems?[11] When our sages dictated this three-times-a day ritual, they intended that we interrupt our daily schedule to ensure a consistent awareness, for ourselves and for others.

I didn't comprehend the above in a vacuum. It also didn't penetrate at home, nor when relaxing on vacation, nor even while reading the mass literature on prayer. Rather, I reached this conclusion as a simple soldier in the Israeli Defense Forces. According to the by-laws of the IDF, the army must give each soldier time to daven every day. There are fixed times written into the laws that govern the army: thirty-five to forty minutes for Shacharit, fifteen minutes for Mincha, and fifteen minutes for Maariv.

I remember one instance when my commander became aggravated that in the middle of the day, right in the midst of training, everything had to stop for my fifteen minutes to daven. He therefore approached me with an efficient idea: "Get up every morning at five and I'll give you an hour and a half to daven all three prayers at once!"

While I was explaining that each prayer had to be recited within a prescribed time period, I began to understand that the sages had ruled precisely against my commander's thinking. The sages wanted us to access this spiritual energy *throughout* the day, at three different times, so that we would always feel that the core values of our spirituality are connected to where we stand at these three intervals during the day, along with where the world around us stands at these times daily. In the words of the famed Rabbi A. Y. Kook:

ראוי שהמציאות הכללית תעורר הטבעה רגשי לב האדם להתפלל. ע"כ תפילת שחרית, ראוי שתעורר לבבו נפלאות וחסדי ה' יתברך הנראים לעין כל בוחן בזריחת השמש. ותפילת המנחה, תעוררהו

---

[11] For more on this theme, see part 4, "Needs: Make It Your Business."

השגחת ה' יתברך וחסדו הנראית בשקיעתה... (עין אי"ה, ברכות
כט:)

It's appropriate that the surrounding reality naturally entice the heart of man to pray. Therefore, the [morning] Shacharit service should entice the heart to the wonders and kindness of G-d that can be seen when the sun rises each day. And the [afternoon] Mincha service should awaken one to the Divine providence and kindness that is seen in the [eventual] setting of the sun…and since one is praying according to the reality and hour of that moment, his prayers are not stagnant and fixed…. (*Ein Aya*, Berachot 29b)

The "service of the heart" is indeed impinged on by this ordinance of the sages. But while the heart may not always be there, your essence as a Jew, your religion – in a world very much devoid of religious sensibility – is on your agenda three times daily.

It's not easy – not physically, and not emotionally. It means coming before the Master of the Universe, right from the hustle and bustle of your office or home, and saying "*Baruch Ata Hashem*" – not "G-d in heaven," but "*Baruch Ata*," blessed are You right here! In the middle of the hectic chaos of your day, you succeed in allowing G-d and the fundamental values of Judaism to penetrate into your life.[12]

---

[12] See more on this theme in part 4, "*Hashem Sefatai Tiftach*: An Innovative Addition and Nobody Screams 'Reformer'?"

Summary

In order to ensure that the core beliefs of a Jew remain an integral part of our consciousness, the sages established set times and texts for prayer. While there is a real price we pay in replacing a heartfelt, spontaneous prayer with a fixed one, the sages created a system in which we would be *annoyed* and interrupted each day a few times, so that G-d would be inserted and connected to our day, at least three times a day.

Daven – with the Mindset of a Baby

While the goal of this book is to "pray your age," I admit that there is one exception to that goal, and that concerns the mindset of a Jew when he comes before G-d in prayer.

My rebbe, Rav Amital, *z"l*, used to say quite often that when coming before G-d in prayer, תתפלל כמו ילד קטן, "Pray like a child." While I never had a chance to ask what he meant, allow me to offer the following explanation. We've explained that while the concept of prayer dates back to our forefathers, the very particular times of prayer correspond to the times that the daily sacrifices were offered in the Temple. This parallel between the sacrifices and prayer dictates yet another law regarding prayer:

בקומו להתפלל, אם היה עומד בחוץ לארץ, יחזיר פניו כנגד ארץ
ישראל ויכוין גם **לירושלים ולמקדש ולבית קדשי הקדשים.**
היה עומד בארץ ישראל, יחזיר פניו כנגד ירושלים ויכוין גם
למקדש ולבית קודש הקודשים.
היה עומד בירושלים, יחזיר פניו למקדש ויכוין גם כן **לבית**
קדשי הקדשים.
היה עומד אחורי הכפורת, מחזיר פניו **לכפורת.** (שולחן ערוך,
אורח חיים צד:א)

When one stands to pray, if one is standing in the Diaspora, one should face Israel and should also have intent toward *Yerushalayim, the Temple, and the Holy of Holies*.

If one is standing in Israel, he should face Yerushalayim, and he should also have intent toward *the Temple and the Holy of Holies*.

If one is standing in Yerushalayim, he should face the Temple and also have intent toward *the Holy of Holies*.

If one is standing on the other side of the Kaporet [the divider between the Holy and the Holy of Holies in the Temple] he should face the *Kaporet*. (Code of Jewish Law, OC [*Orach Chaim*] 94:1)

As we can see, it's not just the times that we pray, but the direction that we face that is aligned with the Temple's Holy of Holies. And beyond time and place, we see that our *intent* when praying should lead us toward Jerusalem, the Temple, and the Holy of Holies.

Similarly, when the Code dictates the mindset and posture of a Jew during the silent Amida, one's private audience with G-d, it uses a Temple-oriented analogy:

צריך שיכוף ראשו מעט, שיהיו עיניו למטה לארץ, ויחשוב **כאילו עומד בבית המקדש** ובלבו יכוין למעלה לשמים. (שולחן ערוך, אורח חיים צה:ב)

One must bend one's head slightly downward, so one's eyes are looking to the ground; and *one should imagine that one is standing in the Temple*, and in one's heart, one should have intent heavenward. (*Code of Jewish Law*, OC 95:2)

It's no wonder that we should be focusing on the Holy of Holies. After all, it is the place that the *kohen gadol* entered to "meet" with G-d, and thus, it seems obvious that we who are about to meet with G-d in prayer should focus on that place.

So what's inside that makes the Holy of Holies so suitable to have a rendezvous with G-d?

When the *kohen gadol* enters this holiest place on earth[1] once a year, what does he see? In front of him, till the destruction of the First Temple,[2] was the holy Ark containing the Tablets. We have no evidence that the Ark was ever opened, and thus just one thing stared the *kohen* in the eye when he entered: the two *Keruvim* (cherubim), resting above the Ark.[3]

These two figures had a peculiar facial image, as Rashi records:

כרבים: דמות פרצוף תינוק להם. (רש"י, שמות כה:יח)

Keruvim: They had the face of a baby. (Rashi, Shemot 25:18)

So, the *kohen gadol* enters the holiest place on the holiest day of the year, and the faces of babies are in there with him, sharing this holy meeting with G-d:

ונועדתי לך שם ודברתי אתך מעל הכפרת מבין שני הכרבים אשר על ארן העדת... (שמות כה:כב)

I will rendezvous with you there, and I will speak with you from atop the Ark cover from between the two cherubim that are upon the Ark of the Testimony.... (Shemot 25:22)

---

[1] Mishna Kelim 1:9.
[2] *Mishneh Torah, Hilchot Avodat Yom Hakippurim* 4:1.
[3] Shemot 25:18–20.

What's going on? Do we really want the holiest representative of the Jewish people to be looking at two baby faces on this holy day?

I'd like to suggest an interpretation I heard in the name of the late Reb Shlomo Carlebach.[4] According to Reb Shlomo, there are three qualities children possess that should be part of the *kohen gadol*'s mindset in the Holy of Holies – and by extension our mindset, as we must focus on the Holy of Holies during prayer.

The first quality is *total faith and security*: If babies aren't hungry, dirty, or in pain, then they're entirely happy. They don't get depressed or "a bit" out of sorts. They either cry when things are bad, or they're *totally* fine! If their basic needs are looked after, they will be absolutely content. When the *kohen gadol* enters the Holy of Holies, or when we stand before G-d in prayer, entering G-d's holy sanctum,[5] we must put our entire faith in G-d, with nothing deterring us from that total and utter sense of security. We shouldn't be half happy, sort of there, or semi-focused, but rather we must feel certain that we have nothing to fear, as we are in the hands of G-d.

Thus, it's no surprise that the Code states:

המתפלל...יחשוב כאלו שכינה כנגדו; ויסיר כל המחשבות הטורדות אותו עד שתשאר מחשבתו וכוונתו זכה בתפלתו. (שולחן ערוך, אורח חיים צח:א)

---

[4] Heard from my student, Rabbi Ariel Shalem. The sources quoted are my own.

[5] There are many sources indicating that prayer occurs in the holy sanctum. The Zohar, for example, states that one must cover his head and eyes during prayer in order "not to see the holy presence of G-d" (Va'etchanan 260b), a notion codified in the *Mishna Berura* (91:6). Rashi asserts that the reason that one must cover oneself during prayer is to "appear standing before the King in awe and trepidation" (Berachot 24b, s.v. "*aval l'tefilla*"). See also the difference of opinion as to how to step back following the silent Amida (Yoma 53b) as dependent on being on the "right side" of G-d.

> One who is about to pray…should conceive of the
> holy presence of G-d standing before him; he should
> *remove any thoughts that disturb him, till his mind*
> *and intent are pure to pray.* (*Code of Jewish Law*, OC
> 98:1)

If we want to pray, we must be like babies – utterly present with
G-d, feeling totally secure, without any outside force in there
with us. Every year, we express this sentiment when we chant the
chapter of Tehillim that is customarily recited by many from Rosh
Chodesh Elul through Sukkot:[6]

כי אבי ואמי עזבוני וה' יאספני: (תהלים כז:י)

> Because my mother and father have left me, and G-d
> will protect me. (Tehillim 27:10)

The second element that we want to take with us into prayer is
total dedication. When babies are hungry or dirty, nothing can
stop them from crying till they're looked after. Their dedication
to their goal consumes them, and they use all the means at their
disposal till they get what they want.[7] As we get older, so many
"logical" excuses tend to prevent us from reaching our true goals,
be it excuses, naysayers, or pessimism. Thus, when we approach
the Holy of Holies during prayer, we must be totally dedicated to
our goal of praying and pleading for the Jewish people and the
world, *with nothing deterring us.*

And so says the Rambam regarding *the* climax of prayer during
the year – the blowing of the shofar on Rosh Hashana:

---

[6] *Mishna Berura* 581:2.

[7] This psychological perspective on young children led the Rama to view a
young child's needs as tantamount to that of someone not dangerously ill,
allowing various leniencies, such as asking a non-Jew to do something on
Shabbat that would be forbidden for a Jew (*Code of Jewish Law*, OC, Laws
of Shabbat 276:1).

אע"פ שתקיעת שופר בראש השנה גזירת הכתוב רמז יש בו, כלומר, "עורו ישנים משנתכם, ונרדמים הקיצו מתרדמתכם, וחפשו במעשיכם וחזרו בתשובה וזכרו בוראכם. **אלו השוכחים את האמת בהבלי הזמן** ושוגים כל שנתם בהבל וריק אשר לא יועיל ולא יציל, הביטו לנפשותיכם". (משנה תורה, הלכות תשובה ג:ד)

Even though the blowing of the shofar on Rosh Hashana is a decree from heaven, it has a hidden message, namely: "Wake up, you who are sleeping, from your sleep, and you who are slumbering, arise from your slumber; consider your actions, return to G-d, and remember your Creator. *Those who forget the truth through passing follies*, and spend the entirety of their years with useless nonsense that won't help them – look to your souls." (*Mishneh Torah, Hilchot Teshuva* 3:4)

Just as when the shofar blows, when praying we hold onto this quality of babies to regain total dedication to what we really want to achieve for our souls, and to disconnect ourselves from the "nonsense" of time that deters us from achieving our goals.

In addition to absolute security and dedication, there's one more quality that we want to hold onto from babyhood: the ability to be *totally over it*. After crying hysterically over whatever made it cry, a baby quickly gets over the matter, smiling and playing as if nothing had happened! No grudge, no hard feelings, but rather utterly forgotten! When standing in prayer, we imitate those babies in the Holy of Holies by being totally over any hard feelings we may have and starting anew with G-d, just like after truly repenting:

כמה מעולה מעלת התשובה: אמש היה זה מובדל מה' אלהי ישראל..., צועק ואינו נענה...ועושה מצות וטורפין אותן בפניו..., **והיום הוא מודבק בשכינה**...צועק ונענה מיד...ועושה מצות ומקבלין אותן בנחת ושמחה...., ולא עוד אלא שמתאוים להם. (משנה תורה, הלכות תשובה ז:ז)

> How amazing is the value of true repentance: yesterday
> he was separated from G-d, Lord of Israel…praying
> and not being answered…doing mitzvot and having
> them be thrown back at him…and today he is *totally
> connected to the holy presence of G-d*…praying and
> being answered…doing mitzvot which are received
> with favor and joy…and are even yearned for….
> (*Mishneh Torah, Hilchot Teshuva* 7:7)

Yom Kippur is a day of atonement, and thus a new beginning.
When the *kohen gadol* sees those babies, he is to start anew with
G-d, without any past feelings or past grudges.

The famous Covenant between the Pieces,[8] which states that
we will be enslaved for four hundred years and yet emerge as
a free nation that will live in the Holy Land, includes a small,
seemingly unimportant, detail: we will emerge from Egypt "with
great wealth."[9] This point is repeated years later to Moshe at the
onset of his tenure as G-d's representative to free the Jews,[10] and
when the time of departure arrives, the Jews do indeed take goods
from the Egyptians,[11] as G-d commanded them.[12]

We can well understand that the Jews shouldn't leave empty-
handed. But why mention it hundreds of years beforehand to
Avraham? Why is this detail significant enough to be revealed to
Moshe as part of the master plan, when the ten plagues and the
splitting of the sea don't merit mention?

Rabbi Jonathan Sacks answers beautifully: In leaving Egypt
the Jews were becoming free, but they would not be truly free if
they were still holding a grudge against the Egyptians. Thus, the
taking of their long-overdue salary ensures that they can march

---

[8] Bereishit 15:9–21.
[9] Ibid. 15:14.
[10] Shemot 3:22.
[11] Ibid. 12:35.
[12] Ibid. 11:2.

from servitude to freedom without harboring any grudges against their former masters.[13]

When we are about to pray, we must enter into G-d's sanctum with no grudges, but rather totally immersed in our job: pleading for the betterment of the Jewish nation and world.

Therefore it is no surprise that the messianic age, a time when we will return to the Temple and its *Keruvim*, has within it the prophesy of...children:[14]

הנה אנכי שלח לכם את אליה הנביא לפני בוא יום ה׳ הגדול והנורא
והשיב לב אבות על בנים ולב בנים על אבותם... (מלאכי ג:כג-כד)

Behold I am sending the prophet Eliyahu to you before the great and awesome day. And he shall return *the hearts of the fathers to their children and the hearts of the children to their fathers.* (Malachi 3:23–24)

Summary

As we face the Holy of Holies three times a day, the place in which two faces of babies adorned the top of the Holy Ark, let us not forget to be in the mindset of children:

- Totally secure
- Totally dedicated
- Totally without grudges!

---

[13] http://www.chiefrabbi.org/tag/hate/#.UMSbjeT2Xh4.
[14] Malachi 3:23–24.

What Happened to the *Yasher Koach* Culture?

There are those who suggest that shuls bring out the worst in people – the fights over various honors, the complaints from those who were insulted and those who weren't honored enough, the politics, and more. On the other end, there are aspects of a shul experience that actually bring out the very opposite. One of those positive aspects of shul life is a commonly used phrase: *yashar koach*, or its close relative *"shekoyach."*[1]

Literally, the phrase means *"go straight to strength."* However, within the context of the prayer service, it's generally meant as a sort of "Jewish" congratulations upon receiving one of the many honors in the synagogue, or facilitating a part of the service on behalf of those congregated there.

I would submit that such a salutation is a *huge* exaggeration – after all, what did the fellow do?

Reciting a blessing before and after the reading of the Torah? Any trained Bar Mitzva boy could do that!

Leading the services? Aside from the High Holiday services, the text is pretty much the same every day, so what's the big deal?!

In my opinion, that's exactly the point: We are living in a world where the normative salutations of "Hello, how are you?"

---

[1] In Sephardic communities, the usual salutation is *"chazak u'varuch"* (be strong and blessed).

are often followed by "I wanted ask a favor...." When was the last time we just said hello for no reason? When did we last greet the people walking by us on the street, for no apparent reason than to simply acknowledge them?! Indeed, I believe that this is a "vanishing buffalo" in our culture, as we typically walk along with either earphones or a phone to our ear, not even noticing others walking by.

As technology develops further, it seems that we will need people less and less. With the advent of the internet, we no longer need bankers, or travel agents, or even supermarkets. When we don't need people, why bother acknowledging them?

It's not that difficult to receive an *aliya* or lead services. And yet, we still say "*yashar koach*," which is basically saying one thing: "I acknowledge you!" In our place of worship, as we pray to achieve our goals, we say "*yashar koach*"; we simply acknowledge the other, offering salutations to total strangers that just happened to receive an *aliya* at our minyan. This is a beautiful part of shul life. We recognize that another Jew has been called up to the Torah, or to be precise, we simply recognize his existence rather than ignore it!

Indeed, we find this dictated, in another context, in a fascinating Mishna:

הוי מקדים בשלום כל אדם. (משנה אבות ד:טו)

You should offer your salutations first to *every person*. (Mishna Avot 4:15)

Notice how the Mishna advised offering a mere hello without knowing the person. Quite the contrary; it should be said to "every person."

Rabbi Yochanan ben Zakai,[2] one of our great Jewish leaders, had many merits. And yet, when the Talmud lists the unique traits

---

[2] Rabbi Yochanan ben Zakai was the *nasi*, the president of the Jewish people. He lived during the destruction of the Second Temple and led the Jewish

of many of the great tannaitic rabbis, it chooses to mention the following about this illustrious leader:

> אמרו עליו על רבן יוחנן בן זכאי **שלא הקדימו אדם שלום מעולם** ואפילו נכרי בשוק. (ברכות יז.)

> They said about R. Yochanan ben Zakai that never did anyone *succeed to offer their salutations to him first*, not even the non-Jew in the marketplace. (Berachot 17a)

Far from aspiring to be "popular," Rabbi Yochanan ben Zakai had other amazing other traits as well:

> אמרו עליו על רבן יוחנן בן זכאי: מימיו לא שח שיחת חולין, ולא הלך ארבע אמות בלא תורה ובלא תפילין, ולא קדמו אדם בבית המדרש ולא ישן בבית המדרש... ולא מצאו אדם יושב ודומם אלא יושב ושונה... ולא אמר הגיע עת לעמוד מבית המדרש חוץ מערבי פסחים וערבי יום הכפורים... (סוכה כח.)

> They said about R. Yochanan ben Zakai: He never engaged in idle speech in his life, nor walked four *amot* without [learning] Torah and without tefillin on his head, and never did anyone get to the study hall before him, and never did he fall asleep in the study hall.... And never did someone find him doing nothing, but rather he was always sitting and learning.... And never did he say, "It's time to stop learning and go home," except for the eve of Pesach and Yom Kippur.... (Sukka 28a)

---

people at this critical time, enacting laws to enable Judaism to endure and flourish without the Temple. See Rosh Hashana 29b, 30a–b, 31b; Beitza 5b; and Sanhedrin 41a.

This great man, who seems to have never deviated from his holy work of learning G-d's Torah and influencing others with its teachings, *still had time to say hello* to everyone who passed by.

Indeed, the small "*yasher koach*" seems to revert back to these old-world values, so needed in today's world.

Relationships are not just a give-and-take. Relationships are built on the fact that you feel important – without any other motive. You're walking down the street, you see someone, and you wonder who is going to say hello first. It might be awkward if you wait, but it's uncomfortable for you to speak first.

Why don't you *just say hello* despite it being artificial? It shows that you value that person for just being a person. And one can well imagine the feeling on the other side: "I was just walking along and someone greeted me!" "I just got an *aliya* and someone acknowledged it!"

This isn't just a considerate mode of behavior. In my opinion it is a pure halachic concept, based on the mitzva of *levaya*, of escorting a guest a few steps out of your door after you host them. In the golden words of the Rambam:

מצות עשה של דבריהם לבקר חולים, ולנחם אבלים, ולהוציא המת, ולהכניס הכלה, וללוות האורחים... **שכר הלויה מרובה מן הכל**, והוא החוק שחקקו אברהם אבינו ודרך החסד שנהג בה, מאכיל עוברי דרכים ומשקה אותן ומלוה אותן, וגדולה הכנסת אורחים מהקבלת פני שכינה...**ולוויים יותר מהכנסתן**. אמרו חכמים **כל שאינו מלוה כאילו שופך דמים**. (משנה תורה, הלכות אבל יד:א-ב)

There is a positive commandment from our sages to visit the sick, to comfort the bereaved, to accompany a body to burial, to bring a bride to her wedding canopy, and to escort guests.... *The reward for escorting guests is greater than all the above*, and it is the law ordained by Avraham our forefather and the kindness he offered, feeding the passersby and

offering them a drink and escorting them. Hosting
guests is greater than receiving the holy presence
of G-d...and *escorting guests is even greater than
hosting them!* Said our sages: *Those who don't escort
their guests are considered as if they have shed blood.*
(*Mishneh Torah, Hilchot Avel* 14:1–2)

According to the Rambam, escorting guests is greater than
bringing a body to burial, or providing assistance for a marriage,
and even than "receiving the holy presence." But all I do is to
walk them a few steps out the door, and that is the greatest mitzva
of the list?

The answer lies in the essence of this particular mitzva. At
the point when you walk someone out your door, you don't need
them anymore; your meal together is over, and you've hopefully
taken care of what you needed to look after.

But now, when all is done, you escort your guests out to show
that you acknowledge their importance, even when you don't
need them. You walk them out your door to acknowledge the fact
that they are alive, and that you value their very existence!

Allow me to illustrate this with the following story, told by
Rabbi Moshe David Tendler about his illustrious father-in-law,
Rabbi Moshe Feinstein, *z"l*:

My *shver* [Rabbi Moshe Feinstein] would come to us
in Monsey on Motza'ei Yom ha-Kippurim and stay
until two weeks after Simchas Torah. That was his
time to himself, when no phone calls or visitors were
allowed in. Only one person was allowed into the
house on Chol ha-Mo'ed Sukkos and that was Rav
Ya'akov [Rabbi Ya'akov Kamenetsky, *z"l*]. He would
come in and sit with my *shver* for two hours chatting
and laughing the whole time like two little boys – not
talking about Torah or politics, but rather reminiscing

about the Old Country together. Then, twenty minutes after Rav Ya'akov left, my shver would come to me and say, *"M'darf geyn bazuchn Reb Yankev"* (We have to visit Rav Ya'akov). We drove over and my shver would come in and wish him *a gut yontef* and then leave. Why? It was part of rabbinic protocol: you came to me, so I have to go to you in turn. Hitler did not kill all the Jews, but he destroyed our culture. There is no remnant of that old-time European ethos in this generation.[3]

Indeed, the mitzva of escorting guests teaches that even when your visit is over, and your business (be it a good meal, a meeting, etc.) is done, you must escort your guest just to acknowledge his very existence.

When a dead body is found between two cities, and the murderer is unknown, the leaders of the town closest to the body must facilitate the ceremony of *egla arufa*,[4] in which they break the neck of a heifer and state "Our hands did not shed this blood." But what exactly are the leaders testifying to? What are they declaring that they didn't do?

Says Rashi,

וכי עלתה על לב שזקני בית דין שופכי דמים הם? אלא לא ראינוהו
ופטרנוהו בלא מזונות **ובלא לויה**. (רש״י, דברים כא:ז)

Did anyone actually think that the elders of the Jewish court were murderers? Rather [they testified that] "we didn't see him and allow him to walk off without food *and without escorting him*." (Rashi, Devarim 21:7)

---

3   http://www.kolhamevaser.com/2010/08/an-interview-with-rabbi-dr-moshe-d-tendler/.

4   Devarim 21:1–9.

Indeed, just acknowledging another's presence is vital! So vital that the leaders attest to their innocence from this unsolved murder – by declaring that they had fulfilled the mitzva of escorting a guest, and did not ignore a strange face in the city.

Our sages commented that גדול הכנסת אורחים מהקבלת פני השכינה, "showing hospitality to guests is greater than receiving the holy presence of G-d."[5] So though we can enumerate many flaws within a shul, how beautiful it is that in the holy synagogue itself, we demonstrate the most extreme "hospitality" by showing every individual how important they are by just being there.

I remember a *Sesame Street* song from my childhood. The chorus was "You're alive, yes, you're alive." Let us acknowledge that people are alive, and implement this *Yasher Koach* culture in our lives outside the walls of the shul as well.

Summary

Thank G-d, the *"yasher koach"* culture lives on in the synagogue, where *we simply acknowledge one another's existence*, and it's my hope that this will spread far beyond those narrow confines to the people that we pass throughout our day. Let's make sure that the *yasher koach* culture doesn't just stay in shul!

---

[5] Midrash Tehillim, *mizmor* 18. The proof text is the episode in which G-d appears to Avraham and while G-d is speaking to him, he sees guests and leaves the presence of G-d to show them hospitality (Bereishit 18:1–3).

 Part II

A Jew at a Minyan

The Quandary of Praying in a Group

The minyan is a basic component of Jewish life, but it has its share of problems. We've already discussed how davening is supposed to be *avoda she'balev*, "service of the heart." So, how exactly can I speak from my heart – in a group? After all, my heart feels differently than yours, and rarely do two people feel exactly the same way at a given moment. How can my lips express my heart's innermost feelings if the minyan is moving at a different pace than I am?

Add to that the fact that the Hebrew of the siddur is not a spoken language, even in Israel![1] If you take the time to read the translation, you will inevitably fall behind and then have to rush in order to say the silent Amida with the minyan.[2] How can it be

---

[1] See Abudraham, *Tikun Hatefillot v'Inyaneihem, shaar* 2: ויש לך לדעת כי לשון התפלה הוא מיוסד על לשון המקרא...., ומלות מעטים יש שלא נמצא להם יסוד במקרא ולכן אביא להם יסוד מהגמרא – "Know that the language of prayer is the Hebrew of the Bible..., and for the few words that are not taken from biblical Hebrew I will bring a source from the Talmud." Based on this, the *Kitzur Shulchan Aruch* (14:11) brings the law from the Code (OC 53:4) that a *chazan* must be one who regularly reads the Bible, explaining, כדי שיהיו הפסוקים שבתפלה סדורים, "so that he will be proficient in the verses brought in the prayers."

[2] The *Code of Jewish Law* (OC, chapter 52) details which prayers should be skipped in order that one pray the silent Amida with the congregation.

"the service of the heart" if you don't understand the words, and if when trying to understand them you end up having to speed up?

We've already discussed how a set text is the antithesis of spontaneity. This problem is compounded when we daven in a minyan, because in order to "go with the flow" we feel obligated to stick to the text, and not wander off adding in our own personal additions and innovations. Aside from not having the time to add in your personal prayers, the minyan also creates silent peer pressure – it seems to the onlooker that everyone is praying "normally" by just reciting the text, while you are challenged with being the lone soldier doing it differently. And even if you have the inner conviction to pray genuinely, there's always that friend waiting to engage you in conversation....

And finally, are the prescribed times for the local minyan always at the most convenient time for your own "service of the heart"? Inevitably, this will not always be the case.

These difficulties could have been avoided by davening privately at home. You would be able to express your heart's desires at your own pace, and in the language you prefer, without interruptions or distractions.

Establishing set prayers already challenged heartfelt prayer. It seems that Chazal further complicate this by ruling that we should daven in a minyan!

Moreover, I can attest from personal experience that trying to maintain a daily minyan of ten men in a small community is a challenge I don't wish on anyone! After four years in Halifax, NS, I can state unequivocally that keeping up a daily minyan is one of the hardest halachot to maintain, much more than having accessible kosher food, maintaining an *eiruv* and *mikva*, and filling your classes with listeners!

It is an ongoing challenge to reconcile praying in a minyan with the critical value of "service of the heart," and I am far from offering a full solution to this problem. But just like any attempt to learn and understand the laws of the Torah, we have a tradition

from the great tanna Rabbi Yishmael that דברי תורה לא יהו עליך חובה
ואי אתה רשאי לפטור עצמך מהן, "The words of Torah shall not be to
you like a debt [to be paid off quickly and thus dispensed with],
and you have no excuse to exempt yourself from toiling in them."[3]
Therefore, let us attempt to understand the law of minyan better,
in the hope that understanding will help us reach the emotional
experience of davening even when praying in a Minyan.

Summary

Lack of spontaneity, peer pressure, distractions
– the problems with a minyan are many. Let's
engage in the laws of prayer to see if despite the
difficulties we can use minyan to deepen our
prayer experience, and our relationship to the
community at large.

---

[3] Menachot 99b.

# A Group Effort That Helps Me

"Come make a minyan," "Where can I *chap* a minyan?" "Are you Bar Mitzva yet?" Thus call fellow Jews to one another frequently throughout the year.

Let's quote the source of these statements from the Code:

ישתדל אדם להתפלל בבית הכנסת עם הציבור, ואם הוא אנוס שאינו יכול לבוא לבית הכנסת, יכוין להתפלל בשעה שהציבור מתפללים, והוא הדין בני אדם הדרים בישובים ואין להם מנין, מכל מקום יתפללו שחרית וערבית בזמן שהציבור מתפללים... כשעומד עם הצבור אסור לו להקדים תפלתו לתפלת ציבור...ולא יפרוש מן הציבור אפילו לעסוק בדברי תורה. (שולחן ערוך, אורח חיים צ:ט-י)

One should do everything possible to pray in a synagogue with a *tzibur* [ten men over Bar Mitzva] and if one is unable to come to the synagogue, then he should pray at the same time that the *tzibur* is praying. And this is the law for people who live in small settlements which don't have a minyan; they should at least pray Shacharit and Maariv at the precise time that the *tzibur* is praying.... When one is with the *tzibur*, one is forbidden from uttering one's prayer before that of the *tzibur*...and one should not separate oneself from the *tzibur* even for the sake of learning Torah. (*Code of Jewish Law*, OC 90:9–10)

Why do we value praying with a *tzibur* so highly? In a word, we are promised that G-d never despises the prayer of a minyan:

מאי דכתיב, "ואני תפלתי לך ה' עת רצון" (תהלים סט:יד)? אימתי עת רצון? בשעה שהצבור מתפללין... תניא נמי הכי, רבי נתן אומר: מנין שאין הקדוש ברוך הוא מואס בתפלתן של רבים? "הן אל כביר ולא ימאס", וכתיב: "פדה בשלום נפשי מקרב – לי" וגו'. אמר הקדוש ברוך הוא: כל העוסק בתורה ובגמילות חסדים ומתפלל עם הצבור – מעלה אני עליו כאילו פדאני, לי ולבני, מבין אומות העולם... (ברכות ח.)

What does it mean when it states "And my prayer is to you, G-d, at the time of yearning" (Tehillim 69:14)? When is "the time of [G-d's] yearning"? When the *tzibur* is praying…. A *beraita* supports this idea: R. Natan says: How do we know that G-d doesn't repulse the prayers of the many? As it says, "The great G-d will not repulse," and it says, "He has redeemed my soul in peace from being close to me." Said G-d: "Whoever busies himself with Torah and acts of kindness and prays with the congregation, from My perspective, it is as if he has redeemed Me and My children from the hands of the nations." (Berachot 8a)

And in an even clearer expression:

כיון דאיכא צבורא דמצלי – לא מדחי. (עבודה זרה ד:)

When there is a *tzibur* praying, G-d doesn't shove it away. (Avoda Zara 4b)

So there you have it: G-d, so to speak, *must* listen to the prayer of a quorum of ten!

Why is this the case? What is minyan all about?

When you're davening in a minyan, everyone present is at a different level of concentration and devotion to prayer. There are those who have intense *kavana* (focus), but there are others who have less or none at all. There are some people in the minyan who have to get back to work, while others have all the time in the world. Some are on vacation and are as calm as the sky on a sunny day, while others are ultra-tense, going out of their way to try to devote a bit of time and concentration. People daven at different speeds, with different spiritual energies – and by davening together *we create a cohesiveness* that ensures that the Jewish nation properly beseeches G-d every day to look after the needs of the world.

Davening with a minyan is a *group effort*. As a group, we each have our strengths and weaknesses, our different merits. Some have *kavana* in certain parts of their Amida and others have *kavana* in other parts. This way, a genuine prayer, *covering all loose ends*, is brought before G-d each day. As explained beautifully by Rabbi Yehuda Halevi:

אבל היתרון לקהל מכמה פנים... ואפשר שיש ביחידים ההם מי שיתפלל במה שיש בו הפסדו... ומפני כן קבעו לנו שיתפלל היחיד תפלת הצבור, ושתהיה תפלתו בצבור בעוד שיוכל לא פחות מעשרה, כדי שישלים קצתם מה שיחסר בקצתם בשגגה או בפשיעה, ויסתדר מהכל תפלה שלמה בכונה זכה. (ספר הכוזרי ג:יט)

The advantage of the community is great for a number of reasons...and it could be that the individual has disadvantages.... Therefore they [the sages] enacted that the individual pray with the congregation [i.e., in a minyan] and this congregation should not be less than ten people, so that some of them can "make up" what others omit, either inadvertently or intentionally, and from it all a complete, genuine prayer will emerge. (Kuzari 3:19)

The idealistic notion that every person has adequate prayerful intention for himself doesn't work all the time. You can be in the shul, say the words, do the motions…and thirty seconds after you finish the Amida, ask yourself what you just prayed for. How often do you have no recollection of what was on your mind when you stood, just moments ago, before the Almighty!

Indeed, we are human. Since the service is regulated in both content and time, it's only natural for there to be a prayer with no feeling; there will be times when we won't have any *kavana*. The words get boring, the place you daven in gets boring, and your head, more than once, is just "not there." However, when you're in a minyan, *you're covered*.[1]

You are covered by others who have a better, clearer mind-set to pray that day, and in turn, by seeing the group surrounding you in prayer, it will hopefully improve your own intent. This is precisely how the Ran explains why the *chelbena*, a foul-smelling spice, was included among the eleven spices that made up the *ketoret hasamim*, the incense:[2]

---

[1] This idea led the Chatam Sofer to a radical conclusion, based on the mystical Zohar (Parshat Noach 69b), regarding the Talmud's statement that "when one prays for someone ill one need not mention his name, as it states [regarding Moshe praying that G-d heal his sister Miriam from *tzaraat*] 'G-d, please heal her'" (Berachot 34a). The Chatam Sofer writes that we need not mention the individual's name in order that he or she not "stand out" in front of G-d, for then G-d will also look at the individual's many sins and shortcomings (Chatam Sofer, *Chidushim*, Nedarim 40a). In other words, if you consider yourself so special and unique, G-d will relate in the same way to you when you are judged (see Rosh Hashana 17a). See also the interpretation of the Malbim regarding the Torah's promise that "there will be no plague among them" when the people are counted by giving the annual half-shekel for the Temple, rather than by being counted individually. Malbim notes that a plague could come if each person were separated and counted individually (Malbim, Shemot 30:12).

[2] Kritot 6a.

וזהו העניין הנרמז בחלבנה הנכנסת בסמני הקטורת, כי עם היות
ריח החלבנה מצד עצמה בלתי נאותה, אפשר שיהיה לה כח לעורר
ולהוציא איכויות הסמים האחרים... וכן על צד המשל, אם ימצאו
בכלל אחד, פרטים בעלי חיסרון מאשר יכביד עליהם...בהמצאם
בתוך הכלל, יעוררו כוחותיהם למה שראוי בפעל הזה ומה שצוותה
בו התורה. (דרשות הר"ן, הדרוש הראשון)

And this is the issue that was hinted in the *chelbena*,
which was included in the *ketoret*: even though its
odor, by itself, is far from being appropriate, it could
be that it had the power to bring out the positive
qualities of the other spices.... The analogy being,
that if there are individuals who possess weaknesses
that place an onus on the others…when they are with
others their own strengths begin to come to fruition in
a crowd of people and they can now fulfill what the
Torah commands. (*Derashot of the Ran, drush* 1)

This understanding may help explain a law regarding *chazarat
hashatz*, the *chazan*'s repetition of the Amida:

אמר להם רבן גמליאל: לדבריכם, למה שליח צבור יורד לפני
התיבה? אמרו לו: כדי להוציא את שאינו בקי. אמר להם: כשם
שמוציא את שאינו בקי – כך מוציא את הבקי. (ראש השנה לד:)

Said Rabban Gamliel to them: According to your
position, why does the *chazan* "go down" before
the pulpit [in order to recite the *chazarat hashatz*]?
They said to him: In order to fulfill the obligation for
those who don't know [how to pray]. He said to them:
Just like he fulfills the obligation for those who don't
know, so too he fulfills the obligation for those who
do know. (Rosh Hashana 34b)

It's easy to understand this ancient enactment of the sages for
those who couldn't pray, whether it's due to the lack of printed

texts before the invention of the printing press, or the inability to read them. But why continue with this practice today when these two reasons are no longer relevant?

Even more perplexing is the codification of the Rambam:

ואחר שיפסיע שליח ציבור שלש פסיעות לאחוריו ויעמוד, מתחיל ומתפלל בקול רם מתחילת הברכות להוציא את מי שלא התפלל, והכל עומדים ושומעים ועונין אמן אחר כל ברכה וברכה, בין אלו שלא יצאו ידי חובתן **בין אלו שכבר יצאו ידי חובתן.** (משנה תורה, הלכות תפילה ונשיאת כפיים ט:ג)

After the *chazan* takes three steps back and stands, he begins [the *chazan*'s repetition] and prays out loud from the beginning of the blessings in order *to fulfill the obligation on behalf of those who didn't yet pray.* And all stand and listen, and answer amen after each blessing, be it those who have not yet fulfilled their obligation [i.e., have not yet prayed by themselves], or *be it those who already fulfilled their obligation.* (*Mishneh Torah, Hilchot Tefilla u'Nesiat Kapayim* 9:3)

If I already prayed, why do I need to "stand and listen"? After all, with regard to other mitzvot, this doesn't apply! For example, if I already made Kiddush on a Friday night, I don't need to "stand and listen" to my neighbor who does so five minutes later! Similarly, if I have already shaken my *lulav*, there is no reason for me to "stand and listen" to someone who hasn't yet. Why is minyan different?

This strange law is clearly codified:

קהל שהתפללו, וכולם בקיאים בתפלה, אף על פי כן – ירד שליח ציבור וחוזר להתפלל, כדי לקיים תקנת חכמים. (שולחן ערוך, אורח חיים קכד:ג)

> In the case of a congregation that prayed, and all those
> present know how to pray – still the *chazan* repeats
> the service, in order to fulfill the enactment of the
> sages. (*Code of Jewish Law*, OC 124:3)

Why do we need to hear the Amida again when we've already
fulfilled our obligation?

This law may not be for the sake of the *chazarat hashatz* itself
as much as *for our sake!* It is for the people who are physically
present in the minyan, and yet their minds are far away.

We can all be physically at prayer, standing/sitting/shaking
like any davener, and yet we are not praying emotionally or
mentally. But when we daven in a minyan, even when we don't
focus on the entire service, there are others who may. And even
if we were mentally absent during our private recitation of the
Amida, the *chazarat hashatz* gives us another opportunity to
achieve prayerful intention.

In a word, the minyan covers us.

Just like the *kohen gadol* took responsibility for the entire Jewish
people on Yom Kippur, so does the minyan take responsibility for
us today. When you daven in a group, then one way or another,
some sort of authentic *tefilla* will go up to heaven on your behalf.

Therefore, when the Rambam gives ideas as to how to have
a positive judgment on the "days of repentance" between Rosh
Hashana and Yom Kippur, he suggests that we engage, among
other things, in צדקה ומעשים טובים, charity and good deeds. As
we are primarily judged for our relationship with G-d during the
days of repentance, and as even Yom Kippur doesn't forgive one
for the sins that one committed to one's fellow Jew,[3] it's rather
strange that the Rambam would suggest actions in the realm
of interpersonal relationships, rather than in the realm of those
between us and G-d. Explains Rav Meir Simcha of Dvinsk:

---

[3] *Code of Jewish Law*, OC 608:1.

ולכן נהגו להרבות בצדקה ובחסד בימים אלו [הלכות תשובה
להרמב"ם (פרק ג, הל' ד)] כדי להשתרש בתוך כלל אחינו בני
ישראל – הכלל הדבוק לאבינו בשמים תמיד. והוי כמו ילדה
שסבכה בזקנה, דבטלה אל הזקנה, דבטל מינה דין ערלה (סוטה
מג, ב), כן הדבוק בכלל ישראל, נטהר מטומאתו בתוך כלל ישראל
עמנו הדבוקים בה' תמיד. (משך חכמה, ויקרא פרק ח)

And therefore the custom is to give much charity
and engage in loving kindness during these days
(*Mishneh Torah, Hilchot Teshuva* 3:4) in order to
have firm roots within the general community of the
Jewish people, the community that [as a community]
is always connected to G-d. Just as when a new
branch is grafted onto an old one, the young branch
is nullified from its *orla*,[4] so too all of the Jewish
community is purified from its defilement if they
are within the general community of the Jewish
people, who are always connected to G-d. (*Meshech
Chochma*, Vayikra 8)

Interestingly, the power of the minyan extends even to those who
aren't present:

אלא...לא פטר רבן גמליאל אלא עם שבשדות. (ראש השנה לה.)

Rather...Rabban Gamliel said that [praying on one's
own at the same time as the congregation prays in the
synagogue] fulfills the obligation only for those in the
field. (Rosh Hashana 35a)

---

[4] The reference is to the laws of *orla*. The "young" branch is one that has been
growing on the tree for less than three years, and one is therefore forbidden
from deriving any benefit from it; the "old" branch is one that is over five
years old. See Vayikra 19:23–25. In this case, the "young" branch was
grafted onto an "older" branch and the question was whether they could be
eaten.

How can I, as a *chazan* in my shul, fulfill the obligation for someone working in the field?

Here we hit on one of the secrets of the minyan institution: even though I may not be physically present, the prayer in the synagogue affects me. How much more so when I'm physically there, but "not there" emotionally!

Thus, you must even skip parts of the initial service in order to recite your private Amida with the minyan.[5] The Amida is so important that it requires the help of the minyan to fill in your potentially missing intent.

However, in order for this "power of the minyan" to work for you, *you have to feel connected and part of the congregation.* This explains why the Rambam obligated not just being in the room, but rather that we must "all stand and listen, and answer amen after each blessing." If you are connected to the people around you, then they can assist you when you are in need of assistance and in turn you assist them in their time of need. If you form relationships with the people around you and help them – providing meals after a birth, paying a *shiva* call, or any other chesed – then you become part of that community.

This notion is beautifully expressed by a law that the *Mishna Berura* states. A person may pray for his own needs, provided he mention his request as part of the general needs of the Jewish people:

ויכול להתפלל על חולים ברפאנו ויאמר, "רפא נא פלוני בן פלוני רפואה שלמה בתוך שאר חולי ישראל". (משנה ברורה קטז:ג)

And one can pray for those who are sick in the blessing of *refa'einu*, saying, "Grant this person, ben that person, a complete recovery among the others who are sick within the Jewish people." (*Mishna Berura* 116:3)

---

[5] *Code of Jewish Law*, OC 52:1.

What's the significance of this formula? If you're davening for a specific personal need, why not just state your personal need and leave the general needs of the Jewish people out of it? At the doctor's office, I tell the doctor my problem with the door securely closed behind me – I don't stand in the waiting room and declare, "My throat hurts among the many Jewish people who have sore throats"!

The Talmudic discussion concerning the proper phrasing of Tefillat Haderech, the prayer said before one embarks on a journey, may help us in understanding the above law:

ואמר רבי יעקב אמר רב חסדא: כל היוצא לדרך צריך להתפלל
תפלת הדרך. מאי תפלת הדרך? "יהי רצון מלפניך ה' **אלקי**
שתוליכני לשלום ותצעידני לשלום" וכו'. אמר אביי: לעולם לישתתף
איניש נפשיה בהדי צבורא. היכי נימא? "יהי רצון מלפניך ה' **אלקינו**
שתוליכנו לשלום" וכו'. (ברכות כט:-ל.)

And said R. Yaakov in the name of R. Chisda: Anyone who embarks on a journey must pray Tefillat Haderech. What is Tefillat Haderech? "May it be Your will, *my* G-d, that *I* shall go in peace, and that *I* shall walk in peace...." Said Abaye: Rather, you should *always intertwine yourself with the general populace.* What should you say? "May it be Your will, *our* G-d, that *we* shall go in peace and that *we* shall walk in peace...." (Berachot 29b–30a)

When we make personal petitions to G-d, we must be concerned with the well-being of the Jewish people and the entire world. True, we may know about the specific needs of ourselves and our loved ones, but *true prayer is about pleading to G-d to ensure the well-being of the Jewish people.*

After all, if your son or daughter is sick, why should your request make it through the "iron curtain"[6] between us and heaven, all the way up to the ears of G-d? Rather, the petition we make is a request on behalf of the entire Jewish people, with our personal petitions reflecting our personal knowledge of the need that the request pertains to. In principle, we want to pray for the needs of the entire Jewish people and world, but since that is impossible, we focus on what is close and personal to us.

If this would not be the case, there would be a situation in which I am praying for myself and my family only, and at times, this would come at the expense of others. For example, if you hear sirens and see ambulances in your neighborhood as you walk home, and pray to G-d, "Let it not be someone in my house," you are implying that you would be ok with it being…someone else in the neighborhood! After all, your sole point of departure is you![7]

However, if you daven in a minyan and look around the room, it will help *you* daven for the welfare of the Jewish people. The guy next to you may have a cold, the woman on the other side of the room may need a job, the guest may need a better salary – when praying in a minyan, you can have the proper intent for almost every blessing. *Even if you don't need it, someone else does*, and together all the needs of the Jewish people and the

---

[6] See Berachot 32b: אמר רבי אלעזר: מיום שחרב בית המקדש נפסקה חומת ברזל בין ישראל לאביהם שבשמים, שנאמר, "ואתה קח לך מחבת ברזל ונתתה אותה קיר ברזל בינך ובין העיר" (יחזקאל ד:ג) – "R. Eliezer said: From the day the Temple was destroyed, an iron wall separates between Israel and their Father in heaven, as it says, 'As for you, take an iron pan and set it as an iron wall between you and the city' (Yechezkel 4:3)."

[7] Perhaps this is the reason that the Talmud (Berachot 54a) states that a prayer asking to change something that already happened (e.g., praying for a boy once the woman is already pregnant, praying to enter a city in peace once the person has already arrived) is a תפלת שוא, a prayer "in vain," both because it is useless to pray about something that has already transpired, but also, homiletically speaking, because a prayer that is just focused on you is "in vain"!

world are being brought, by a collective effort, before G-d. But not less importantly, when you will be in need, those around you will pray on your behalf!

This is why the Tefillat Haderech is in plural, as are the rest of our prayers.[8] This understanding may explain the following halacha as well:

> יש מי שאומר שכשמוסיף בברכה לצורך יחיד, **לא יאריך.** (משנה
> ברורה קיט:ב)

> Some say that when one adds a personal request to a blessing, *he shouldn't make it too long.* (*Mishna Berura* 119:2)

It's not about Moshe or Leah, it's about the well-being of the Jewish people as a whole, and therefore it's not appropriate to elaborate too much on just one person.

What emerges is a beautiful synthesis. We pray for the entirety of the Jewish people, and yet, as the Rav commented, since it's very difficult to relate to a number like "six million," we can and should focus on the needs that we can see and feel. In his words:

> People respond to the story of an individual personal tragedy more readily than to a national tragedy on a large scale. The Midrash on *Parshat Noach* (Gen. Rabba 33:5) recounts that Rabbi Akiva came to the city of Ginzak to collect money for charity. He expounded on the story of the flood when all humanity was drowned. The people did not cry; they were not touched; they did not respond emotionally. Then Rabbi Akiva told them the story of Job, and

---

[8] See *Code of Jewish Law*, OC 119, as to when you can revert from the plural to the singular.

they immediately broke out in tears and complied
generously with Rabbi Akiva's request."[9]

Therefore, the next time you pray in a minyan, look around the
room for just a minute and contemplate what's on the personal and
communal agenda before uttering the words so that the prayers
will help you, together with the entirety of the Jewish people. So
suggests the Code:

ישהה שעה אחת קודם שיקום להתפלל, כדי שיכוין לבו למקום.
(שולחן ערוך, אורח חיים צג:א)

One should devote one hour before praying in order
to have the proper intent before G-d. (*Code of Jewish
Law*, OC 93:1)[10]

And if that hour is not available, the *Mishna Berura* has a more
lenient view:

ומיהו: זה לחסידים. ולשאר עם די בשעה מועטת שישהה קודם
שיתחיל שהוא כדי הילוך ח' טפחים. (משנה ברורה צג:א)

Rather, this is for the extra pious. But for the masses,
it's enough to devote at least the time needed to
walk eight handbreadths [approximately sixty-four
centimeters]. (*Mishna Berura*, 93:1)

Concentrate on the specific needs of those around you. It will
help your our own davening and *kavana*. Or, take a newspaper
and review the world's troubles. See what challenges the Jewish
people and world are facing today. When you read about corrupt
leaders, let it cause you to have more *kavana* in *hashiva shofteinu*,

---

[9] *Koren Mesorat HaRav Kinot* (Jerusalem: OU Press/Koren Publishers, 2010),
page 443.

[10] See the great importance given to this time period in Berachot 32b.

"restore our judges." When you hear about Jerusalem, G-d forbid, being "up for grabs," concentrate in the blessing of *li'Yerushalayim ircha*, "may You return to Your city, Jerusalem."

We need to foster a sense of community amongst us – not just for the community, but for you.

Summary

With all its faults, praying in a minyan has a major benefit. Since we can't always have intent for the words we say, the others "cover us" by virtue of their private intent, or by virtue of the *chazan*'s repetition of the service. When we all pray for our personal needs, *the needs of the Jewish people are collectively brought before the Almighty's throne*. Through the group effort of the minyan, an authentic prayer will hopefully pierce the heavens.

Praying with a Minyan – for Better and for Worse

It's well known that a minyan is made up of the magic number 10. How do we know that we need specifically ten? The source is shocking:

מנא הני מילי?

אמר רבי חייא בר אבא אמר רבי יוחנן: דאמר קרא, "ונקדשתי בתוך בני ישראל" (ויקרא כב:לב) – כל דבר שבקדושה לא יהא פחות מעשרה.

מאי משמע?

דתני רבי חייא: אתיא תוך תוך, כתיב הכא "ונקדשתי בתוך בני ישראל", וכתיב התם "הבדלו מתוך העדה" (במדבר טז:כא). ואתיא עדה עדה, דכתיב התם "עד מתי לעדה הרעה הזאת" (במדבר יד:כז). מה להלן עשרה, אף כאן עשרה. (מגילה כג:)

What is the source for [the law that ten men make up a minyan]?[1]

Said R. Chiya ben Abba in the name of R. Yochanan: The verse states, "And I shall be sanctified

---

[1] The Gemara's question is referring to a teaching in the Mishna (Megilla 4:3): אין...עוברין לפני התיבה ואין נושאין את כפיהם ואין קורין בתורה ואין מפטירין בנביא...פחות מעשרה – "We do not...have a *chazan* lead services, nor have the *kohanim* bless the people, nor read publicly from the Torah, nor read the haftara...when there are less than ten." For further details, see the *Code of Jewish Law*, OC 55.

in the midst of the children of Israel" (Vayikra 22:32) – any form of verbal sanctity shall be said in the assemblage of ten.

How do you deduce this law from there?

As R. Chiya taught: We derive it from a *gezeira shava*[2] from the term "in the midst." It says here, "And I shall be sanctified in *the midst* of the children of Israel," and it says elsewhere, "Separate yourselves from *the midst* of this *eida* [assemblage]" (Bamidbar 16:21).

And we derive a *gezeira shava* from the term *eida*, as it says there, "How long shall I bear with this evil *eida*..." (Bamidbar 14:27). Just like there [Bamidbar 14] the verse is referring to ten, so too here it means ten. (Megilla 23b)

The source for reciting words of sanctity with a minyan is derived from *one of the most grievous sins in the history of the Jewish people, the sin of the spies*. Twelve spies were sent on a touring mission of Israel; ten of them returned with a slanderous report about the land. G-d punished the ten spies with death, and decreed that all who believed their slanderous report would die in the desert over the course of the next thirty-eight years; only their children would be privileged to enter the Holy Land.[3] It is in this context that the above verse is uttered. Referring to the *ten* spies that began this chain effect of tragedy, G-d states "How long shall I bear with this evil *eida*..." (Bamidbar 14:27).

These ten men are the source of sanctity? Out of the entire Bible, we couldn't have found a more positive verse that implied a better group of ten men? These men are responsible for delaying

---

[2] A *gezeira shava* is a Talmudic principle in which laws are derived from a term based on its appearance in two different contexts.

[3] Bamidbar 14:1–5, 26–29.

the plan to enter Israel for thirty-eight years; due to their "report," the Jewish people "cried that night" concerning the prospect of entering such a land, and these tears developed into the most tragic day in the Jewish calendar, Tisha b'Av:

וכתיב, "ותשא כל העדה ויתנו את קולם ויבכו העם בלילה ההוא"
(במדבר יד:א). אמר רבה אמר רבי יוחנן: אותה לילה ליל תשעה
באב היה. אמר להם הקדוש ברוך הוא: "אתם בכיתם בכיה של חנם
- ואני קובע לכם בכיה לדורות". (תענית כט:)

It is written, "And all the congregation lifted up their voice, and cried; and the people wept that night" (Bamidbar 14:1). Said Raba in the name of R. Yochanan: That night was the night of Tisha b'Av. Said G-d to them: "You cried for no reason – therefore I am decreeing crying on this day for all generations." (Taanit 29b)

How could it be that these ten are the source of our holy minyan? Moreover, the second verse quoted above ("separate yourselves from the midst of this *eida*") refers to those who followed Korach's rebellion against Moshe's leadership. Is this too the best choice for our holy quorum of ten?

I believe the Gemara is sharing a basic truth about life in a community: *a community is imperfect!* The Jewish people are far from being angels all year,[4] and therefore part and parcel of our yearly cycle is a Yom Kippur to atone for those very misgivings, sins, and imperfections.

Yom Kippur does not occur only if necessary. Our eternal Torah states matter-of-factly, כי ביום הזה יכפר עליכם לטהר אתכם מכל חטאתיכם לפני ה' תטהרו, "Because on this day atonement will be

---

[4] *Code of Jewish Law* (OC 610:4) mentions that many of our once-a-year practices on Yom Kippur are there in order for us to resemble angels, but this is indeed just once a year.

made for you, to purify you from all your sins, before G-d you shall be purified."[5] On this day, throughout the generations, there will be a *need* for Yom Kippur each year as "an *eternal* statute."[6]

The Jewish people are not angels, but humans who fall and at times sin. As I heard endless times from my revered rebbe, Rav Yehuda Amital, *z"l*, in the name of the Rebbe from Kotzk, G-d commands that אנשי קודש תהיון לי, "holy people you shall be for Me!"[7] – holy *people*, with their imperfections. "It is as if," says the Kotzker Rebbe, "G-d is saying, 'I have enough angels – now I want holy *people.*'"

The source for minyan refers to imperfect, yet potentially holy people.[8] You may be perfect (at least in your eyes), but the Jewish people still have many imperfections. *When you connect to the Jewish people as a whole, you will inevitably be connecting yourself to imperfections.* And if you want to "use" the Jewish people in order to hear the Torah reading or say Kaddish, you have to be prepared to deal with the problems and challenges that come with being part of the nation.

Our tradition repeatedly teaches us that a community is not complete without its imperfections.[9] Regarding praying on a fast day, for example, our sages make a startling declaration:

---

[5] Vayikra 16:30.

[6] Ibid. 29, 30.

[7] Shemot 22:30.

[8] This discussion relates to the dispute between the sages of the Talmud regarding whether we are called "children of G-d" even after we sin (Kiddushin 36a). Similarly, there is a dispute recorded in which a Sadducee suggests that G-d's holy presence departs from the midst of the Jewish people when they are impure, while Rav Chanina disagrees (Yoma 56b–57a). A myriad of sources suggest that the Jewish people remain Jews, with G-d's holy presence, even when they fall and sin (Berachot 7a; Rosh Hashana 17b; Sanhedrin 44a, 111a–b, among many others).

[9] Many Hasidic works have quoted that the root of the term ציבור (community) – צ.ב.ר. – stands for צדיקים, בינוניים, רשעים – the righteous, the mediocre, and the sinners! See, for example, *Likutei Moharan* 1:55.

כל תענית שאין בה מפושעי ישראל אינה תענית, שהרי חלבנה
ריחה רע, ומנאה הכתוב עם סממני קטרת. (כריתות ו:)

Any fast day that doesn't include sinners of Israel is
not considered a fast day [from a halachic perspective],
as the *chelbena* [one out of the eleven spices that
comprised the daily *ketoret* sacrifice] has a bad odor,
and still the verse counted it among the spices of the
ketoret. (Kritut 6b)

Picture the scene: A fast is declared in response to a tragedy that
has befallen the Jewish people. All have come together, after
thorough introspection, to plea before G-d. *And the prayer service
can't begin...until sinners are also present!*

This idea also appears in a more familiar source – the opening
passage of the Kol Nidrei prayer, recited on the holiest day of the
year:

על דעת המקום ועל דעת הקהל, בישיבה של מעלה ובישיבה של
מטה, אנו מתירין להתפלל עם העבריינים. (על-פי השולחן ערוך,
אורח חיים תריט:ט)

With the consent of G-d, and with the consent of this
congregation, by the authority of the heavenly court
and by the authority of the earthly court, *we declare
that it is lawful to pray with sinners.* (Based on the
Code of Jewish Law, OC 619:9)

Could we think of nothing better to say at the onset of this exalted
day than declaring that we are planning to share the space of our
holy sanctuary with sinners?

But that's exactly the point. G-d promised that on this day of
Yom Kippur, the *community* of Israel would be forgiven! Never
was such a promise made for the individual.[10] Thus, if you, an

---

[10] For an elaboration on the distinction between atonement for the individual

individual, want to be forgiven, you have to connect yourself to the community – and that unquestionably includes sinners. And yet, this very group has the aforementioned divine promise of forgiveness, as well as the uncanny group benefits of a minyan. In the words of Rabbi Meir Simcha of Dvinsk:

ולכן "אמרו אליו כל תשא עון", היינו שכלליות האומה תשא כל העון שלא ישתייר אפילו שוגג. "וקח טוב", פירוש, חשבוהו כזכויות. (משך חכמה, הפטרות, פרשת וילך)

And therefore the [prophet Hoshea] states, "Say: You shall carry all iniquity," meaning that the entire Jewish nation will "carry" all the iniquity, so that not even an accidental sin will remain.[11] And thus "take good," which means that [the sins] will be turned into mitzvot. (*Meshech Chochma*, Haftarot, Parshat Veyeilech)

The very opposite of this obligation is the legacy of one of the worse places on earth,[12] so bad that G-d had to destroy it[13] – Sedom. So state our sages:

---

versus for the community on Yom Kippur, see *Al Hateshuva*, Harav Yosef Dov Halevi Soloveitchik, trans. and ed. Pinchas Peli (Torah Education Department of the World Zionist Organization, 1975), pages 69–101.

[11] The verse is part of the haftara from the Shabbat between Rosh Hashana and Yom Kippur, known as "Shabbat Shuva" (the Shabbat of Return). The Shabbat is named after the first words of its haftara, which read, "Return, O Israel, to the Lord your G-d, for you have stumbled in your sins. Take words with you and return to the Lord. Say, 'You shall *carry all iniquity and take good...*'" (Hoshea 14:2–3). The *Meshech Chochma* is attempting to explain the italicized words, as one usually doesn't "*carry*" iniquity" but rather should try to get rid of it!

[12] Bereishit 13:13.

[13] Ibid. 19:24–25.

אנשי סדום אמרו: "הואיל ומזון יוצא מארצנו, וכסף וזהב יוצא
מארצנו, ואבנים טובות ומרגליות יוצאות מארצנו, אין אנו צריכין
שיבאו בני אדם עלינו! אין באין עלינו אלא לחסרנו! (תוספתא
מסכת סוטה, ג:יב)

The people of Sedom said: "Since the food comes
out of our land, and the gold and silver come from
our land as well, and beautiful, expensive jewels
and diamonds come from our land, we don't need
people to come to us [from the outside]! They are
only coming to take away [from all our resources].
(Tosefta, Sota 3:12)

The people of Sedom felt that they had no reason to share, as they
had it all, and had no intention to be connected to those coming
from less perfect societies. The Jewish legacy, on the other hand,
is quite the opposite.

The idea that the community is only complete with its
imperfections is also expressed in one of Chazal's oft-quoted
statements: כל ישראל ערבין זה בזה, "All Israel are guarantors for one
another." This is not just a beautiful idea or sermon; it has legal
implications as well. For example:

תני אהבה בריה דרבי זירא: כל הברכות כולן, אף על פי שיצא,
מוציא, חוץ מברכת הלחם וברכת היין. (ראש השנה כט.)

Said Ahava, R. Zeira's son: Regarding all of the
blessings, even though one has fulfilled one's
obligation, one can enable others to fulfill their
obligations, except for the blessing over wine and
bread. (Rosh Hashana 29a)

On a typical Friday night, even if I already recited Kiddush for
myself, I can recite it again for someone who hasn't yet heard
Kiddush. But isn't this the same Torah that prohibited uttering

G-d's name in vain?[14] Let the Jew who can't recite Kiddush take care of him or herself!

But as Rashi explains:

שהרי כל ישראל ערבין זה בזה למצות. (רש"י, ראש השנה כט.)

After all, "all Israel are guarantors for one another" for mitzvot. (Rashi, Rosh Hashana 29a)

The concept of *areivut*, of being a guarantor, allows me to repeat G-d's name again and again, even for a Jew who doesn't care about the mitzva of Kiddush! Since we are guarantors for each other, my own observance of the commandment is incomplete as long as there is a Jew out there whose obligation remains unfulfilled, in the very same way that one who is a guarantor for a debt can be asked to pay it as long as the borrower is unable to.[15] In the words of the Chafetz Chaim:

...דדוקא בברכת המצות שכל ישראל ערבין זה בזה, וכשחבירו אינו יוצא ידי המצוה **כאלו הוא לא יצא**. לכן יכול לברך אפילו מי שאינו חייב בברכה זו. (משנה ברורה, סימן ריג:יד)

...Specifically regarding the blessings over mitzvot, as "all of Israel are guarantors for one another," such that when one's fellow Jew did not fulfill a commandment, *it is as if he didn't fulfill his either.* Therefore he can recite the blessing again, even though he himself is not obligated in the mitzva at this time. (*Mishna Berura* 213:14)

The Rambam doesn't mince words when speaking about those who separate themselves from the community:

---

[14] See Devarim 6:13, 10:20; Nedarim 10a; Temura 3b; *Mishneh Torah, Hilchot Shevuot* 12:11; *Code of Jewish Law*, YD (*Yoreh Deiah*) 334:37.

[15] See Ritva, ad loc.

הפורש מדרכי צבור, ואף על פי שלא עבר עבירות אלא נבדל מעדת
ישראל ואינו עושה מצות בכללן ולא נכנס בצרתן ולא מתענה
בתעניתן אלא הולך בדרכו כאחד מגויי הארץ וכאילו אינו מהן –
אין לו חלק לעולם הבא. (משנה תורה, הלכות תשובה ג:יא)

One who separates from the ways of the community,
even though he doesn't sin but rather separates from
the Jewish people, and doesn't perform mitzvot
together with them, or identify with their hardships,
or fast on their fast days, but rather goes about his
business like one of the non-Jews of the land, as if
he is not part of them – that person has no share in
the world to come. (*Mishneh Torah, Hilchot Teshuva*
3:11)

Indeed, the most important woman in the realm of prayer, Chana,
wife of Elkana, pleaded before G-d for a son by stating, ונתת לאמתך
זרע אנשים, "And You shall give your servant *a seed of people*."[16]
While Chana promised that her son would be devoted totally to
G-d, as he would be part of the staff of the Tabernacle, her plea in
this strange phrase is explained as follows:

מאי זרע אנשים? ...ורבנן אמרין: זרע שהוא מובלע בין אנשים...
(ברכות לא:)

What is "a seed of people"? ...The majority opinion
of the sages is that he would be part of the people
[literally, "swallowed up" by the people]. (Berachot
31b)

---

[16] I Shmuel 1:11. The first chapter of Shmuel (which is also the haftara for the
first day of Rosh Hashana) records Chana's heartfelt prayer in the Mishkan
(Tabernacle), after being barren for many years. The manner in which she
prayed that day is the most important source for the way we pray the silent
Amida each day. Almost every law that governs the silent Amida is deduced
from the manner in which Chana prayed, including the way we move our
lips yet speak silently (Berachot 31a–b).

Chana did not envision a "religious worker" separated from the people, or above the people, but rather part of them.[17] It's no wonder that Chana's plea is the source of many of the laws that govern prayer.

The Rambam's statement may explain a fascinating passage found in Tosfot. The Talmud states: אל ישאל אדם צרכיו לא בג' ראשונות ולא בג' אחרונות, "One should not petition G-d during the first and last three blessings of the Amida,"[18] as these are reserved for praise and thanksgiving, respectively. Therefore, it's rather surprising that during the Ten Days of Repentance, from Rosh Hashana through Yom Kippur, we add into the first three blessings prayers that are unquestionably petitions:

זכרנו לחיים, מלך חפץ בחיים, וכתבנו בספר החיים, למענך, אלוקים חיים.

Remember us for life, King Who desires life, and write us in the Book of Life, for Your sake, the G-d of Life.

מי כמוך, אב הרחמים, זוכר יצוריו לחיים ברחמים.

Who is like you, Father of Mercy, Who mercifully remembers His creatures for life.

How are we allowed to insert petitions in the first three blessings during the Ten Days of Repentance?

Tosfot answers as follows:[19]

---

[17] See I Shmuel 7:16, which relates that Shmuel would go each year on a major trip around the country to serve the people, rather than stay in the confines of the Tabernacle and wait for them to approach him. The sages actually explained that this was the crux of the difference between Shmuel and his sons, who took over after him: while they awaited the people in their "Eiffel Tower," he went to them, as he felt part of them (Shabbat 55b–56a).

[18] Berachot 34a.

[19] Ibid.

פי' ר"ח ורבינו: האי דוקא ליחיד, אבל צרכי צבור שואלין. ולכך אנו
אומרים "זכרנו..." ויעלה ויבא בהם. ותדע דדוקא יחיד קאמר שהרי
עיקר ברכות אחרונות צרכי צבור הם.

Explained Rabbeinu Chaim and Rabbeinu: This
law [prohibiting petitions in the first and final three
blessings] only applies to the individual petition,
but the needs of the community can be prayed for.
Therefore, we insert *zochreinu* and *yaaleh v'yavo* in
[these blessings]. You should know that this is only a
prohibition for the individual, since the essence of the
final blessings are the needs of the entire congregation.

Tosfot concludes that if we are asking for the *group*, then it's okay
to petition G-d anywhere, even in the first and last three blessings
of the Amida. Though you certainly are praying for your own life,
the prayer is expressed in the plural – *zochreinu*, "remember us."
The focus of the prayer is communal, and as part of the group
you are entitled to beseech G-d in ways that you couldn't when
staying in your own bubble. Hopefully, you will then receive all
the group benefits as well.

The Rambam seems to be making this same point when he
distinguishes between what he terms *"tefilla im hatzibur,"*[20]
praying on your own within a congregation (i.e., your own private
Amida recited within a quorum of ten men), versus the *chazan*'s
repetition, which he defines as *"tefillat hatzibur,"* the prayer *of the
congregation*:

תפלת הציבור נשמעת תמיד ואפילו היו בהן חוטאים אין הקדוש
ברוך הוא מואס בתפלתן של רבים, **לפיכך צריך אדם לשתף עצמו
עם הציבור**, ולא יתפלל ביחיד כל זמן שיכול להתפלל עם הציבור...

---

[20] See, for example, 6:2: המתפלל עם הציבור לא יאריך את תפלתו יותר מדאי, "One
who prays with the *tzibur* shouldn't extend his private prayer too long."

וכל מי שיש לו בית הכנסת בעירו ואינו מתפלל בו עם הציבור
נקרא שכן רע. (משנה תורה, הלכות תפילה ונשיאת כפיים ח:א)

The *tefillat hatzibur*, the prayer *of* the congregation, is always accepted [by G-d], and even if the congregation includes many sinners G-d does not repulse the prayer of the many. Therefore, *one should partner oneself with the congregation*, and one should not pray alone as long as one has the possibility of praying with the congregation.... And whoever has a synagogue in the city but does not pray in it with the congregation is called a bad neighbor. (*Mishneh Torah, Hilchot Tefilla u'Nesiat Kapayim* 8:1)

One *chazan* unites the people around one prayer before G-d. By praying with your community, you become part of those offering a prayer that will never be "repulsed" by G-d.

This would further explain an amazing license, given to the grand court called the Sanhedrin, that transformed Jewish life as we know it:

ויש לבית דין לעקור אף דברים אלו לפי שעה...שאפילו דברי תורה
יש לכל בית דין לעקרו הוראת שעה. כיצד? בית דין שראו לחזק
הדת ולעשות סייג כדי שלא יעברו העם על דברי תורה... וכן אם
ראו לפי שעה לבטל מצות עשה או לעבור על מצות לא תעשה
כדי להחזיר רבים לדת או להציל רבים מישראל מלהכשל בדברים
אחרים, עושין לפי מה שצריכה השעה. **כשם שהרופא חותך ידו או
רגלו של זה כדי שיחיה כולו, כך בית דין מורים בזמן מן הזמנים
לעבור על קצת מצות לפי שעה כדי שיתקיימו [כולם]**, כדרך שאמרו
חכמים הראשונים, "חלל עליו שבת אחת כדי שישמור שבתות
הרבה". (משנה תורה, הלכות ממרים ב:ד)

And the court can temporarily annul one of these [rabbinic commandments]...for the court even has the power to temporarily annul a biblical commandment. How so? If a court sees the need to strengthen mitzva observance by instituting a decree aimed at preventing people from violating a biblical commandment.... And similarly, if they see fit to temporarily annul the obligation to fulfill a positive or negative commandment in order to bring the people back to their religious roots or to save many Jews from sinning, they should do whatever is necessary. *Just as a doctor amputates a hand or a leg in order that the entire body survive, so too the court can instruct, in a given scenario, to temporarily transgress the mitzvot, in order that all the mitzvot be [eventually] kept.* This is as our sages said, "Violate one Shabbat in order to keep many more Shabbatot." (*Mishneh Torah, Hilchot Mamrim* 2:4)

Truly amazing! The Grand Court can permit eating pig in order to bring us back to the proper level, just like a doctor can amputate a leg in order to save an entire body! Explains the Radbaz:

כשם שהרופא חותך וכו': אין המשל הזה צודק אלא אם כן **אנו רואין את כל ישראל כאילו הם גוף אחד.** ואף על פי שגופין מחולקין הם, כיון שנשמותיהם ממקום אחד חוצבו הרי הם כגוף אחד כי הנשמה היא עיקר.

"Just like the doctor can amputate...": This analogy can only be correct *if we consider the entire Jewish people as one cohesive body.* Even though they are divided into different bodies, since their souls all come from one source they are like one body, as the soul is the most vital part.

The obligation to pray in a minyan is rooted in ten sinners. Next time we join a minyan, we must remember that we are connecting to the Jewish people, as a whole, who contain many imperfections. We must be willing to connect to them, understand them, and do what we can to fix those imperfections. Then we will be privileged to the "group benefits" that are so priceless:

כיון דאיכא צבורא דמצלי - לא מדחי. (עבודה זרה ד:)

When there is a *tzibur* present, G-d doesn't shove it away. (Avoda Zara 4b)

Summary

Praying with a minyan teaches a Jew to connect to the Jewish people, with all their inevitable problems and challenges. Next time we pray with a minyan, let's remember to come out of our bubbles, and reconnect to the public thoroughfare of the Jewish people despite their shortcomings. When we join with others, even at the expense of our own concentration, and even when connecting to less desirable elements of society, we reap the benefits of the group.

Don't Forget the Individual

When people speak about a successful community, what do they usually mention?

Numbers! We speak of high numbers, be it membership of a synagogue, or participation at events, and we thereby prove our success. On the other hand, low membership and poor turnouts at events will commonly be perceived as failure.

But truth be told, Jewish sources teach that the success of a community is not measured by high numbers but rather by the many *unique individuals* that create the group. Minyan attendance isn't just about the public singing and the *chazan*'s repetition of the Amida, nor the privilege to recite the *devarim she'bi'kedusha*, the parts of the service that may only be recited when ten men are present. Minyan is also about your personal standing before G-d.

Therefore, just as you may have to surrender your personal prayer, by skipping various parts of the service for the sake of saying the Amida with the minyan, so too the *chazan* must not begin the repetition until nine others finish their private Amida and are able to answer amen after his blessings.[1] *The congregation and the chazan must also surrender to the individual.*

This may be why Communism had such an issue with Judaism. On the surface, there is no contradiction between them, and one

---

[1] *Code of Jewish Law*, OC 124:4.

can find many sources for socialism within the Torah. So why was it so crucial for the Communist regime to outlaw any exhibition of Judaism? What fueled Marx's famous declaration that "religion is the opium of the masses"?

Communism did not represent the individual. The term Communism is rooted in the word "commune," which implies that only the *collectiveness* of the country and the party will count, not the individual's personal needs.

We in Judaism have a place both for the individual and for the community, and this synthesis must be upheld despite its complexity. My revered rebbe, Rav Amital, *z"l*, would often illustrate this point through the book of Shemot. In this second book of the Bible, we are transformed from specific families[2] into a nation, as we move from slavery to freedom. This book begins by mentioning each of Yaakov's children by name, even though they have already been listed at the end of the first book of the bible, Bereishit. Rashi explains that they are counted once again in order to show G-d's love of the Jewish people.[3] Rav Amital explained that Rashi is teaching a profound lesson about Jewish communities: a community is made up of individuals. Thus, at the onset of moving from a family to a nation, each individual is counted.

In davening within a minyan, we must be sensitive to this. We dare not just talk about large numbers that frequent our synagogues, but also about the unique individuals who make up those numbers.

Thus, when seeing a large gathering of Jews, we do not bless G-d by saying, "Blessed are You, G-d, Who has fulfilled His

---

[2] The book of Bereishit, which precedes the book of Shemot, begins with the first human beings: Adam and Eve and their offspring in chapters 1–6:7, the family of Noach and their offspring until chapter 11, and then the family of the very first Jews and their offspring from chapter 12 till the end of the book.

[3] Shemot 1:1.

promise to make the Jewish people like the sand of the earth and like the stars above that can't be counted."[4] Rather, we say ברוך חכם הרזים, *"Blessed be He Who knows many wisdoms,"*[5] in the plural, celebrating each individual's uniqueness.

Why did Hashem pick Moshe to lead the Jewish people? The Torah doesn't specify which of Moshe's attributes led to him being chosen over other potential candidates, but Chazal fill in the "missing minutes on the recording":

> כשהיה משה רועה צאן של יתרו במדבר, ברח ממנו גדי אחד ורץ אחריו... נזדמנה לו בריכה של מים ועמד הגדי לשתות. כיון שהגיע משה אצלו אמר לו, "אני לא הייתי יודע שרץ היית מפני שעיף אתה". הרכיבו על כתיפו והיה מהלך. אמר לו הקב"ה, "יש לך רחמים לנהוג צאנו של בשר ודם – חייך, אתה תרעה צאני. (שמות רבה ב:ב)

> When Moshe was shepherding Yitro's sheep in the desert, one little sheep ran away, and Moshe ran after him.... The sheep reached a pool of water and prepared to drink from it. When Moshe caught up to it, he said, "I didn't know you were running away because you were tired [and thirsty]." He put the sheep on his shoulder and walked back. G-d said to Moshe, "You have mercy on the sheep of flesh and blood – I promise that you will be the shepherd for My sheep." (Shemot Rabba 2:2)

---

[4] These are the images G-d uses when He blesses our forefathers (Bereishit 22:17, 32:13, and 26:4). This divine promise is later invoked by Moshe, when G-d "contemplates" destroying the Jewish people as a result of the sin of the golden calf (Shemot 32:13); it is restated on the eve of Moshe's death (Devarim 1:10, 10:22). Finally, one of the curses that will befall the Jewish people if they fail to live up to their mission is that they will be small in number (Devarim 28:62).

[5] Berachot 58a.

For the leader of the Jewish people, Hashem chose a man who looks out for the *individual* sheep, not just the herd at large. The same is written about King David, years later, who was also a shepherd.[6]

As Rav Soloveitchik explained, "Judaism has a different understanding of and approach to the individual. We mourn for the individual even if he or she was not a significant person."[7]

A typical example would be the case of a rabbi who serves in a very small community. Such a community, with hardly enough men to make a minyan, was informed that one of the families had become "too *frum* for the community" and had decided to make *aliya*. What should the rabbi do? Should he deter them from making *aliya* to save the minyan and the community?

My personal opinion is clear: The shul exists to fulfill the spiritual needs of its members. If this family's needs are not being fulfilled in their community, then the rabbi, responsible for the individuals who make up the community, should encourage their *aliya* even though it will hurt the community.

---

[6] I Shmuel 16:11–12. See Shemot Rabba 2:3 for a similar description about King David. According to the midrash, G-d "tested them with small things [e.g., sheep not grazing in the fields of others] and they turned out to be faithful."

[7] *Koren Mesorat HaRav Kinot*, page 443. The Rav is explaining why, in the midst of a series of *kinot* dealing with the destruction of the German communities during the Crusades, there is a *kina* about a simple boy and girl who died during the period of the destruction of the Temple. Also see page 77, where the Rav relates to this theme.

Summary

The shul is for individuals to become inspired and grow, by connecting with others. If the individuals cannot do this, then the community will fall apart. Therefore, we wait for the individual to finish his personal Amida before continuing with the service. This is what the dual laws of minyan teach us: *the individual must have his place* even as we all daven together as part of a bigger whole.

Minyan: The Anti-Egocentric Daily

This is being written in the twenty-first century. When the history of this period will be documented, one of the overriding principals will be but one word: I! The internet lulls into a false sense of self-sufficiency – we can satisfy so many of our needs without asking help of others. Perhaps it's not a wonder that many new technological inventions today have *I* in it – iPod, iPad... Even the one invention called the *We* is spelled *Wii*!

The Jewish world is far from being immune to this egocentricity. Jewish wedding dances can serve as a trivial example – as my rebbe, Rav Amital *z"l*, once commented, "In the past, people would dance at weddings in a circle. Today, each person jumps *alone*!"

Minyan can help us deal with this problem in more ways than one. First, you can't daven without nine others. Although you can recite Korbanot and Pesukei d'Zimra by yourself, the crux of davening requires a minyan. In a minyan, *I* need the *we*.

Furthermore when you have finished, but the *chazan* and/or the majority of the congregation has not, you should wait to proceed to daven together.[1] *This should humble you* – you have to wait for

---

[1] *Code of Jewish Law* (OC 124:4) states that if nine people don't answer amen after each blessing, it is "close to being a blessing in vain."

others to continue with your prayer. Moreover, the law forbidding
a person from walking in front of someone who is in the midst of
the Amida[2] is far more relevant in the synagogue than at home.
Indeed, its frequent practice would force a Jew to be considerate
of someone else's place within the whole.

In the words of Rabbi Shimon Shkop:

ולדעתי מרומז ענין זה במאמרו של הלל עליו השלום, שהיה אומר
(אבות א:יד): "אם (אין) אני לי מי לי, וכשאני לעצמי מה אני?"
היינו שראוי לכל אדם להתאמץ לדאוג תמיד בעד עצמו, אבל עם
זה, יתאמץ להבין שאני לעצמי מה אני. שאם יצמצם את ה"אני"
שלו בחוג צר כפי מראית עין, אז "אני" זה מה הוא. (הקדמה לשערי
יושר)

> In my opinion, this is hinted in the words of Hillel,
> who used to say, "If I am not for myself, who am
> I? And when I am for myself, what am I?" (Avot
> 1:14). In other words, each person should take care
> of himself, and with all that, he should struggle to
> understand that "if I am [just] for myself, what am
> I" – if he reduces his "I" to this narrow radius, just as
> far as his eye can see, then what is this "I" anyway.
> (Introduction to *Shaarei Yosher*)

The most basic parts of the service that require a minyan – Barchu,
Kaddish, and Kedusha – are called *devarim she'bi'kedusha*,
words of holiness.[3] What is the common denominator between
the three? All three require a duet between the *chazan* and the
congregation. Just as a relationship gets built by giving and taking,
by individuals making space for each other, so too in these words
of holiness the *chazan* and congregation come together. Indeed,
the tractate dealing with the forming of a marital relationship is

---

2   *Code of Jewish Law*, OC 102:4.
3   See Berachot 21b; Megilla 23b; *Code of Jewish Law*, OC, chapter 52.

called Kiddushin – holiness. True holiness is when two people interact together, not alone.

As we pointed out, it's preferable to pray in a synagogue with a minyan.[4] However, the *Code of Jewish Law* stipulates:

ואם הוא אנוס שאינו יכול לבוא לבית הכנסת, יכוין להתפלל בשעה
שהציבור מתפללים... וכן אם נאנס ולא התפלל בשעה שהתפללו
הציבור והוא מתפלל ביחיד, אף-על-פי-כן יתפלל בבית הכנסת.
(שולחן ערוך, אורח חיים צ:ט)

And if one is unable to come to the synagogue, then he should pray at the same time that the *tzibur* is praying.... And if he is unable to pray at the same time as the congregation, and he is praying alone, he should still pray in the synagogue. (*Code of Jewish Law*, OC 90:9)

A rather strange story is brought in the Talmud regarding this law:

שנים שנכנסו להתפלל, וקדם אחד מהם להתפלל ולא המתין את
חברו ויצא - טורפין לו תפלתו בפניו, שנאמר, "טרף נפשו באפו
הלמענך תעזב ארץ" (איוב יח:ד). ולא עוד אלא שגורם לשכינה
שתסתלק מישראל, שנאמר, "ויעתק צור ממקמו" (שם). (ברכות ה:)

If two people enter [a synagogue] to pray, and one finishes his prayers and leaves instead of waiting for the other individual – his prayer is thrown back in his face, as it says, "One who destroys his soul in his anger! Shall the earth be abandoned for your sake?" (Iyov 18:4). And moreover, he causes the holy presence of G-d to be removed from the Jewish people, as it says, "And shall the Rock be removed from His place?" (Ibid.). (Berachot 5b)

---

[4] *Code of Jewish Law*, OC 90:9.

Is it so terrible to leave the synagogue while your friend is still praying, when your own prayers are done? Indeed, a synagogue experience should conjure up the very opposite of egocentricity. Praying in a synagogue is designed to counteract our selfishness – a lesson particularly relevant in our time.

Therefore, it's no wonder that the Gemara states:

אמר הקדוש ברוך הוא: כל העוסק בתורה ובגמילות חסדים
ומתפלל עם הצבור – מעלה אני עליו כאילו פדאני, לי ולבני, מבין
אומות העולם. (ברכות ח.)

Said G-d: Anyone who busies himself with Torah and good deeds and prays with the congregation – I will consider it as if he has redeemed Me and My children from the hands of the nations of the world. (Berachot 8a)

Joining a minyan is equivalent to doing good deeds, because in a minyan, we are praying for others as well as for ourselves. More significantly, we can now understand why praying in a minyan is likened to redeeming the Jewish people from captivity: A prisoner sits in his cell, usually feeling very alone. With so much time on his hands, he will likely spend a lot of time lost in thought, and mostly his thoughts will revolve around himself – how *he* will survive, where *he* can sneak another parcel of food, how *he* will make it through the painful interrogations. A free person has the ability to think of others, and thus he is able to help so many others, "chained" in the captivity of their inability to speak to G-d properly.

Summary

Acknowledging the other, when waiting for one to finish the *Amida* and the like, is part and parcel of davening in a minyan. Regular minyan attendance can therefore help us become more considerate and attentive in our relationships to the significant others who are part of our lives.

I'm Part of the Symphony

Anyone who watched *Sesame Street* as a kid will remember the ever-famous song, "Who are the people in your neighborhood? The people that you meet each day!" I would like to end our discussion of minyan with this sentiment, encouraging us to get to know the people in our neighborhood.

The Gemara we quoted in the previous chapter continues with the other side of the coin, speaking of one who does not frequent his local synagogue:

> אמר ריש לקיש: כל מי שיש לו בית הכנסת בעירו ואינו נכנס שם
> להתפלל נקרא שכן רע, שנאמר, "כה אמר ה' על כל שכני הרעים
> הנגעים בנחלה אשר הנחלתי את עמי את ישראל..." (ירמיהו יב:יד).
> ולא עוד אלא שגורם גלות לו ולבניו. (ברכות ח.)

> Said Reish Lakish: Anyone who has a synagogue in his city but doesn't enter it in order to pray is called a bad neighbor, as it says, "Said G-d regarding all the bad neighbors who seized the inheritance that I've bequeathed to My people..." (Yirmiyahu 12:14). And not only that, but he brings exile upon himself and his children. (Berachot 8a)

How is it that when a person merely neglects to enter his synagogue he brings exile upon his family, and if he does pray in the synagogue, it's like he redeemed captives?

Rav Soloveitchik once suggested an explanation of the Gemara based on viewing a symphony orchestra at work. He noticed that some of the musicians worked harder than others, and he wondered if they were all paid equally. Most noticeably, there was one musician who only banged his cymbals three times during the entire performance.

So he approached the conductor following the performance, asked the question, and the conductor replied in the affirmative. "Yes," he said, "all the musicians are paid the same, even though this musician banged his cymbals three times and did not work as hard as the others. Because without him, *the symphony would be incomplete.* His small contribution made the symphony complete!"

This, suggested the Rav, explains the Gemara's declarations. The Gemara does not say that you are a wicked, despicable person if you don't go to shul. Rather, you are a "bad neighbor." We are supposed to work cohesively for the betterment of our people and the world at large. In a minyan, everyone works together. Some contribute their capacity for *kavana*, others their ability to lead services and read the Torah...and the final product is a group effort.[1]

When you daven alone, you think only of yourself. But a minyan creates a new entity. Not one person playing the flute, the other the trombone, and the third the guitar all in their own abodes. Rather, the gathering of different Jews creates a symphony.

Rav Soloveitchik expressed this in halachic terms regarding the distinction between two types of sacrifices: *korban hashutafim*, the sacrifice of many partners, versus *korban hatzibur*, the sacrifice of the entire congregation. Though the former may have tens of thousands of "partners," it will only belong to those partners. In

---

[1] Rabbi Hershel Schachter, *Divrei Harav: Collected Lectures, Insights and Rulings of Rabbi Joseph B. Soloveitchik, zt"l* (OU Press, 2010), 148–149.

contrast, the *korban hatzibur* belongs to the entire entity of the Jewish people:

"קרבן הציבור"...בניגוד גמור לקרבן השותפין שיש לו הרבה בעלים
אין לו אלא בעלים אחד, ממש כמו קרבן היחיד, ומי הוא הבעלים?
הציבור, "כלל ישראל", שאינו על-פי דין הסך הכולל, הצירוף
האריתמטי, של כך וכך יחידים, אלא אישיות ייחודית-עצמית,
מעין חטיבה בפני עצמה..."כנסת-ישראל" כחטיבה אחת. (על
התשובה, 74-75)

> In contradistinction to the *korban hashutafim*, which has many owners...the *korban hatzibur* has but one owner, as if it is a *korban hayachid*, a sacrifice that belongs to one individual. And who is the owner? The congregation, *klal Yisrael*, which is not the sum total, the arithmetic combination of x amount of individuals, but rather one unique, independent personality, an entity unto itself...the people of Israel as one unit. (*Al Hateshuva*, 74–75)[2]

The *korban hashutafim*, like the *korban Pesach*, is a sacrifice that can have many owners. Whoever is not signed on originally cannot partake of the meat of the *korban Pesach* on Seder night.[3] But the *korban hatzibur* is a sacrifice of the entire congregation, just like the twice-daily *tamid* sacrifice, or the famous scapegoat on Yom Kippur that atones for the sins of the entirety of the Jewish people. In these cases it is not relevant to speak of a number of people that are part of the sacrifice, but rather the entire nation as a single entity brings these sacrifices. Thus, says the Rav:

---

[2] Harav Yosef Dov Halevi Soloveitchik, *Al Hateshuva*, trans. and ed. Pinchas Peli (Torah Education Department of the World Zionist Organization, 1975). The essays in *Al Hateshuva* were originally delivered orally by the Rav in Yiddish. A similar idea to that expressed by the Rav can be found in Rav Hutner's *Pachad Yitzchak* on Pesach, *maamar* 33.

[3] See *Mishneh Torah, Hilchot Korban Pesach* 2:1.

הגדרה זו של כנסת ישראל כאישיות עצמית שלמה...היא דפיניציה
(definition) הלכתית מובהקת המסתעפת לכמה עניינים שבהם
אנו מצווים להבחין בין כלל ישראל כצירוף של יחידים לבין כלל
ישראל כאישיות עצמית בלתי מתחלקת. (על התשובה, 76)

This definition of the Jewish people as an independent
entity...is a halachic definition that applies in various
cases in which we distinguish between the Jewish
people as a group of individuals and *klal Yisrael* as an
indivisible entity. (*Al Hateshuva*, 76)

Our prayers are paralleled to the Temple sacrifices; we pray at
the same times that the sacrifices were offered in the Temple. Just
as the *korban tamid* was a *korban tzibur*, so too the prayer of a
minyan is a *tefillat hatzibur*.[4] It is not just the sum total of all our
individual *tefillot* – after all, once we reach the number ten, it
is immaterial whether there are ten or a thousand people in the
room. Rather, the *tefillat hatzibur* is a new entity, so different that
it allows us to recite parts of the service that we couldn't say
alone, such as Kaddish and Torah reading.

This symphony, playing the various "instruments" together, is
indeed far greater than its individual parts, so much greater that so
much more can said and hopefully achieved.

---

[4] *Mishneh Torah, Hilchot Tefilla u'Nesiat Kapayim* 8:1.

Summary

By neglecting the minyan you are considered a bad neighbor, because you are not joining with your community – the "symphony." Conversely, when you do unite with those around you, the symphony will sound better, and even if your own contribution to the music is minimal, you will receive the applause that the entire symphony will hopefully receive from on high.

Part III

Walking toward the Amida

Birkot Hashachar: Don't Let a *Yud* Become a *Vav*

"One of the fundamentals of our faith is expressed in *Fiddler on the Roof*." So I heard from my dear rebbe, Rav Aharon Rakeffet, many times.[1] Indeed, even a first-time observer of that classic would observe that the film contains so much of the Jewish people's core beliefs, not to mention their struggles and hopes.

In one scene of the movie, Tevya tells Golda that he made a match for their daughter with the rather old *shochet*. Golda becomes enraged, as the match was finalized without ever discussing it with her. The fight is followed by the famous song, "Do you love me?"

Golda's response was typical of any Jew: dodge the question. "Do I love you? What do you mean? For twenty-five years I washed your clothes, ironed your shirts, and cooked your food…" But Tevya persists and asks, *"But – do you love me?"*

This entire scene can be analyzed by just two words, Hebrew words that sound very similar to one another, and yet carry different meanings: *shachiach* and *shachuach*.

---

[1] On that note, Rav Rakeffet expressed many times that he personally knows assimilated Jews who returned to Judaism as a result of the song "Tradition" in that movie.

שָׁכִיחַ	שָׁכוּחַ
Shachiach means frequent or common.	*Shachuach* means forgotten.

They sound very much alike, with the only distinction being that the former has a *yud*, while the latter possesses a *vav*, which changes the vowels under it.

I would like to suggest that anything in life that is *shachiach* can easily become *shachuach*. Anything that is frequent and consistent is forgotten, disregarded. That which we encounter daily is not given the proper recognition. On the other hand, the one-time play you're gearing up toward, or the yearly festival that arouses your excitement, is far from forgotten.

The difference between these two words lies in the *yud*, which if extended a bit downward can turn into a *vav*. Writing this word quickly, you can naturally have a *vav* in place of a *yud*. We live under the same roof as our wives and children and see them every day. Precisely because we see them all the time, we forget how special they are, and how vital they are to our existence. When was the last time you told any of them, on a simple Tuesday night, "I love you," "You're special to me," or "I'm going to take care of you"?

For this reason, we begin our davening every morning by ensuring that the *yud* not become a *vav*. We start by reciting *Birkot Hashachar*, the Morning Blessings, in which we thank G-d for various aspects of nature. None of what we mention is extraordinary. We do have distinct blessings for infrequent and extraordinary phenomena in nature, such as thunder, lightning, and rainbows.[2] But Birkot Hashachar celebrate the habitual mundane:

---

[2] Mishna Berachot, chapter 9.

כי מתער, אומר: "אלקי, נשמה שנתת בי טהורה... ברוך אתה ה'
המחזיר נשמות לפגרים מתים". כי שמע קול תרנגולא, לימא:
"ברוך אשר נתן לשכוי בינה להבחין בין יום ובין לילה". כי פתח
עיניה, לימא: "ברוך פוקח עורים"... כי לביש, לימא: "ברוך מלביש
ערומים". (ברכות ס:)

When he gets up, he says: "My G-d, the soul that
You've given me is pure…. Blessed be You, G-d,
Who returns souls to dead bodies." When he hears
the rooster, he says: "Blessed be He Who has given
the rooster the ability to distinguish between day and
night." When he opens his eyes, he says: "Blessed
be He Who opens eyes." …When he gets dressed,
he says: "Blessed be He Who dresses the naked."
(Berachot 60b)

The rooster crows in the morning, you woke up, you can get up
off your bed, you got dressed – none of these are a big deal. They
happen every morning, they're part of our normal routine, we're
used to seeing them – and that is precisely the reason for these
berachot. We dramatize these normal occurrences, *so that we
make sure to express amazement over them*.[3]

Of course, the question is obvious: if we have them all the
time, what makes them so amazing? The answer is rather
simple: think about how you would feel if they were taken away.

---

[3] The Ramban (Pesachim 7b, s.v. "*v'hevei yodeia*") explains that these are not
birkot hanehenin, blessings that we recite after benefiting from particular
phenomena, but rather blessings of praise over the phenomena themselves.
Therefore the blessings do not need to be recited immediately after benefiting
from these phenomena, but rather can be recited at any time. The Ramban's
approach is in contrast to that of the Rambam (*Mishneh Torah, Hilchot
Tefilla* 7:4–9), who identified these blessings as *birkot hanehenin*, and thus
was against the common custom to recite these blessings as one unit in
shul, since one would not be deriving benefit from these phenomena at that
time. Of course, one can suggest that the blessings serve both functions, as
suggested by the Rosh (Berachot 9:23) and Pri Chadash (OC 46:2).

Imagine the day when you can't move due to a bad back. You nurse it during the day and go to sleep at night, with the help of painkillers, awaking the next morning with no problem. Think of the *kavana* you'd have when you say *zokeif kefufim*, the blessing acknowledging G-d for straightening the bent!

Or say you've got bitten by a mosquito in the middle of the night, and your eye swells up and you can't see. Your spouse drives you to the doctor, you take a shot of antihistamine, and a day later you're fine. Think of the *kavana* you'd have when you say *pokei'ach ivrim*, the blessing acknowledging G-d for giving sight to the blind.

The tragedy of the human condition is that we appreciate what we have...when it's gone or taken away. We appreciate our car when it's in the garage for days due to repairs, we miss our kids when they're in camp, and we miss our spouses when we are away from them for a prolonged trip! Birkot Hashachar lift us up, encouraging us to *appreciate what we have – when we have it.*

The hardest thing to appreciate is something that is there all the time. Tevya never told Golda that he loved her because she was always around, she was taken for granted. Birkot Hashachar guard against that, requiring us to verbally acknowledge the daily blessings in our lives.

Therefore, each morning, we fulfill a rather strange halacha regarding these blessings. While the Gemara, as well as the Code,[4] spoke of one hearing the rooster and *then* saying the blessing, or physically getting out of bed and immediately reciting the blessing of straightening the crooked, we today say all these blessings as one unit, regardless of how far we live from the sound of the rooster, or how long ago we got out of bed.[5] Beyond the various

---

[4] *Code of Jewish Law*, OC 46:1.

[5] Ibid. 2. See also the Rama (ibid. 8), who states that even if, for example, one didn't get out of bed that morning (and as such, G-d didn't "straighten the crooked"), one would still say these blessings over the very phenomena, unlike the opinion of the Code (ibid.). However, many Sephardic Jews follow

explanations for this deviation from the original practice,[6] I believe this custom can easily be explained based on the above: since these phenomena are around all the time, and indeed they are not extraordinary in any way, a blessing is in place *anyway.* We don't have to wait for a special occasion to offer a blessing, we can bless someone or something that is around on any ordinary day.

Summary

Don't wait for it to be taken away to verbally appreciate it. Birkot Hashachar remind us to acknowledge all the normal activities that we do every morning. Let's appreciate the precious blessings in our lives every day.

---

the former custom of saying the blessings only after personally experiencing them – see *Kaf Hachaim* 46:49, and *Yalkut Yosef* 46:8.

6 The Rosh (Berachot 9:23) states that this is due to one's hands not being clean till one comes to shul; the Tur (OC 46) suggests, among other things, that this is out of consideration for those who were unable to recite the blessings in Hebrew.

Mizmor l'Toda: Thanks for Nothing – That I Know About

We Jews like very short prayers. We like small pieces of davening, because we can see the beginning and end on less than half a page. Therefore, many Jews look upon Mizmor l'Toda as one of the more favorable parts of the service, even if the custom is to stand for its duration;[1] the entire passage doesn't take up more than four lines in the average siddur.

What is this short prayer all about? The Mizmor l'Toda commemorates the *korban toda*, the thanksgiving sacrifice that was brought in the Temple. The *korban toda* was not an obligatory sacrifice, but rather a voluntary offering brought to thank G-d for being rescued from a dangerous situation.[2] It is similar to the

---

[1] See *Code of Jewish Law*, OC 51, *Shaarei Teshuva* 9. Though the *Shaarei Teshuva* himself seems to be in favor of sitting for Mizmor l'Toda, he quotes the *Be'er Heitev* and others in favor of standing.

[2] This is the more common view, though some felt that it's obligatory in cases in which one was saved from the dangerous situations about to be cited. See the interpretation of Rav Perla to the *Book of Mitzvot* by Rav Saadya Gaon (1:259–260), where he believes this is a point of dispute between Rashi, who felt it was obligatory, versus the Rambam, whose silence indicates that he felt that it wasn't obligatory, and the Tosfot, who says explicitly that it isn't obligatory (*Shita Mekubetzet*, Archin 11b:6).

more commonly known *birkat hagomel*,[3] which we are obligated to recite in certain situations.[4] So states the Code:

ארבעה צריכים להודות: יורדי הים כשעלו ממנה, והולכי מדברות כשיגיעו לישוב, ומי שהיה חולה ונתרפא, ומי שהיה חבוש בבית האסורים ויצא.

מה מברך? "ברוך אתה ה'...הגומל לחייבים טובות שגמלני כל טוב". והשומעים אומרים: "מי שגמלך כל טוב, הוא יגמלך כל טוב סלה". (שולחן ערוך, אורח חיים ריט:א)

Four must thank G-d: those who passed through the seas safely, those who journeyed through the desert and reached human habitation, one who was ill and was healed, and one who was in jail and emerged.

What blessing do you recite? "Blessed be You, G-d, King of the universe, Who bestows good upon the obligated, for You have bestowed good upon me." And all respond: "He Who has bestowed this goodness on you – may He bestow all goodness upon you forever." (*Code of Jewish Law*, OC 219:1)

The reasons for reciting *birkat hagomel* are similar to the reasons for which one brings a *korban toda*.[5] And indeed, it's

---

[3] Many, though not all, see a direct correlation between those who bring a *korban toda*, and those who must say the hagomel blessing – see Rashi, Vayikra 7:12; Semag, positive commandment 85, and certain views brought by Rav Perla (ibid.).

[4] *Code of Jewish Law* 219:1–2, based on Berachot 54b.

[5] Rashi, Vayikra 7:12: "אם על תודה יקריבנו": אם על דבר הודאה על נס שנעשה לו, כגון יורדי הים והולכי מדברות וחבושי בית האסורים וחולה שנתרפא, שהם צריכין להודות – שכתוב בהן (תהלים קז:כא-כב) "יודו לה' חסדו ונפלאותיו לבני אדם" – "If he will sacrifice [the peace offering] as a thanksgiving offering": "If he brings it to give thanks for a miracle that happened to him – such as those who passed through the seas, those who journeyed through the desert, those who were imprisoned, and those who were healed from sickness. All of these people must offer thanksgiving, as it is written, 'They shall thank G-d for His

understandable that we would thank G-d upon emerging safely
from a potentially dangerous situation. But why do we have to
thank G-d, through reciting Mizmor l'Toda, *every day*? We're
not obligated to recite *hagomel* every day, and in the days of the
Temple, we didn't have to bring a *korban toda* every day. Why,
then, is this passage part of the daily prayers?

The answer may lie in our understanding of one word from
the *hagomel* blessing: *chayavim*. In the language of our sages, we
know that the term *chayav* can simply mean "obligated" to fulfill
a command of some sort.[6] But many a time, the word is used in
a context implying liability for a sin. One who bakes bread on
Shabbat, for example, is *chayav* – he must bring a *chatat* sacrifice
to atone for his sin.[7] Similarly, one who eats *chametz* on Pesach
is *chayav* – he incurs the punishment of *karet*, of being cut off
in a premature death from the Jewish people.[8] And throughout
tractate Shabbat, the term *chayav* implies that the individual
has transgressed a biblical Shabbat law, and is now obligated to
bring a *chatat* sacrifice.[9] In a word, *chayav* means that *you've
been convicted of something, and you are obligated to pay the
price*. Indeed, a short comment by the Magen Avraham regarding
Mizmor l'Toda indicates that the term *chayavim* in this prayer
carries this meaning. The Magen Avraham states that a child
under the age of Bar Mitzva should not recite this blessing, since
in doing so he would say the word *chayavim*, yet he is not guilty
of sin at his young age![10]

---

kindness and for the miracles He performs for human beings [and they will
offer thanksgiving sacrifices]' (Tehillim 107:21–22)."

[6] See, for example, Mishna Berachot 9:3, Peiah 1:3, Sheviit 4:8, Challa 1:2.

[7] Sheviit 10:7.

[8] Challa 1:2.

[9] Shabbat 1:1, 2:5, 6:2, etc.

[10] Introduction to OC, chapter 219 in the Code, dealing with the blessing of
hagomel.

Despite being "obligated," or guilty, the blessing states that G-d saved you *anyway*. In the words of the *Mishna Berura*:

"הגומל לחייבים טובות": פירוש: אפילו לאותם שהם חייבים, עם

כל זה גומל להם טובות (משנה ברורה ריט:ד)

"He Who bestows good upon the obligated": This means that even to those who are guilty, G-d still bestows good. (*Mishna Berura* 219:4)

While we've established that we are guilty, we still don't know why. Why would a Jew, just saved from a terrible predicament, be branded guilty? What was his sin?

Allow me to share an idea from Rabbi Yaakov Kamenetsky, *z"l*:

...דכיון שמזכיר "הגומל לחייבים טובות", אם כן הוי ליה כמו

וידוי... ואפשר דתודה גם כן משום וידוי הוא, כלומר "הגיע אלי

יותר ממה שצריך לי". (אמת ליעקב על אורח חיים ריט:ב, עמ' קד)

...Since one says, 'Who bestows good upon the obligated,' it is like he is saying Vidui [the Confession].... And thus it could be that the *toda* is also a confession, in other words, "I got more than I deserved." (*Emet l'Yaakov* on the *Code of Jewish Law*, OC 219:2, page 104)[11]

Indeed, G-d bestows good upon us without our knowledge and we have no idea of what we have to be thankful for. We don't have a clue about what's happening in the world around us, and how many dangers G-d has saved us from. We can go through an ordinary day, blissfully unaware of the miracles occurring all around us.

---

[11] *Emet l'Yaakov* on the four sections of the Code, edited by his son Rabbi Avrohom Kamenetsky (Kisvei Publication, 2000), page 104.

We may hear on the news that our soldiers caught a terrorist before he was able to fulfill his vicious plan, yet similar events happen regularly without making the news. Sometimes we hear about them, sometimes we don't, but our security forces, together with G-d's eternal providence, are always working. Since we're unaware of the myriad situations that we're saved from, it's easy to overlook them. Our ignorance makes it difficult to thank G-d every day for the endless acts of kindness that keep us alive.

And therefore we are guilty – because we did not say "thank you" for all the amazing things that were done each day on our behalf. We failed to acknowledge the incredible daily occurrences that smooth our paths, and therefore we are *chayav*.[12]

Our sages emphasize the importance of acknowledging G-d's hidden miracles in their discussion of the righteous King Chizkiyahu. Chazal criticize Chizkiyahu for not thanking G-d after being saved from the hand of Sancheriv, who encircled Jerusalem in preparation for a war…that never happened:

> חזקיה, שעשית לו כל הנסים הללו ולא אמר שירה לפניך – תעשהו
> משיח? (סנהדרין צד.)

> Chizkiyahu, to whom You did all these miracles yet he didn't sing praise of thanksgiving to You – would you even consider nominating him to become *Mashiach*? (Sanhedrin 94a)[13]

---

[12] One may ask why we still utilize the term *"chayavim"* (liable) in *birkat hagomel* if we give thanks every day. It is possible that since the blessing of *hagomel* predates Pesukei d'Zimra, we don't tamper with the text, even though it is not a blessing per se. See, for example, *Responsa Yechaveh Daat* by Rav Ovadya Yosef (OC 1:43) for the various sources indicating that we do not tamper with the blessings of the Men of the Great Assembly since these sages combined great wisdom with the remnants of prophecy.

[13] For an account of the events themselves, see II Melachim, chapter 19.

Imagine – Chizkiyahu lost his chance to be the *Mashiach* just because he didn't say "thank you." We try to learn from Chizkiyahu's oversight. Each day, we say Mizmor l'Toda – we thank G-d for everything He did unbeknownst to us. In the words of the Eliyahu Rabba:

...ונראה משום דמזמור זה אין אומרים לשם קרבן תודה אלא לשם **הודאה** (בית יוסף). ולעניות דעתי, דעת הבית יוסף דאם היו אומרים לשם קרבן, אסור גם בזמן הזה דמיחזי כשיקרא, כיון שאינו קרב. (אליהו רבה רפא:ט)

...And it seems that this psalm is not said for the sake of the *korban toda* but rather as *thanksgiving*. And in my opinion, it is the opinion as well of the Beit Yosef that if this were said in place of the sacrifice, it would be forbidden to say even today since it would seem like a lie, for the *korban toda* is no longer sacrificed. (Eliyahu Rabba 281:9)

We may not be aware of all the salvations that are done on our behalf, but we must acknowledge them.

And this is the idea behind all of the Pesukei d'Zimra, the Psalms of Praise that we recite daily. The Talmud is bothered by a contradiction between two statements and resolves the contradiction as follows:

אמר רבי יוסי: יהא חלקי מגומרי הלל בכל יום.
איני? והאמר מר: הקורא הלל בכל יום – הרי זה מחרף ומגדף!
כי קאמרינן בפסוקי דזמרא. (שבת קיח:)

Said R. Yossi: May I be together with those who finish the Hallel [thanksgiving prayer] each day.

Can it be so? But didn't Mar say: One who says Hallel every day is a blasphemous act before G-d?

Rather, [R. Yossi's statement] is referring to the Pesukei d'Zimra [Psalms of Praise]. (Shabbat 118b)

Indeed, the special Hallel prayer is reserved for unique days during which unique events and miracles occurred, such as Pesach and Shavuot.[14] But each day, we say the psalms of Pesukei d'Zimra, not to give praise and thanksgiving for the supernatural and unique, but rather to acknowledge the ongoing, so-called "natural" miracles each day that may be unknown to us. And therefore, in the midst of these psalms, we recite Mizmor l'Toda, thanking G-d for the hidden miracles done on our behalf daily.

Interestingly enough, toward the end of the service, between the recitation of Ashrei and u'Va l'Tzion, we insert psalm 20, beginning with the words למנצח מזמור לדוד יענך ה' ביום צרה ישגבך שם אלקי יעקב, "A song to David. May the Lord answer you on a day of distress; may the name of the G-d of Jacob fortify you." Commenting on this psalm, the Tur comments, rather matter-of-factly, that we recite it לפי שיש בו מעניין הישועה, "Because it speaks of salvation"! Even when there is no apparent reason to request salvation, a day is filled with endless dangers we have no idea about, and thus, right before the service is over, we beseech G-d for salvation from all the troubles that may come our way.

And since these hidden, unknown miracles from above will, G-d willing, never cease, the Code states:[15]

שכל השירות עתידות ליבטל חוץ ממזמור לתודה...

...all the songs of praise will be cancelled in the messianic future except for Mizmor l'Toda!

---

[14] See the complete list in Archin 10a, *Mishneh Torah, Hilchot Megilla v'Chanuka* 3:6. The days enumerated are the special holidays of the year, as well as Chanuka. While Purim should have been on the list, as its miracles are unique as well, the Gemara gives three different reasons why we don't say Hallel on that day (Megilla 14a).

[15] *Code of Jewish Law*, OC 51:9.

Summary

We say "thank you" every day for having our days run smoothly and safely. We thank G-d "for nothing" – i.e., for nothing that we know about. Though we aren't aware of the hidden miracles that G-d does for us daily, we acknowledge His silent intervention in our lives.

Ashrei: From A–Z and That's It?

Ashrei, one of our most famous chapters of Tehillim (Psalms). Kids are taught the tune early in life, and the acrostic makes it one of the easier prayers to remember.

It's not incidental that we teach Ashrei to our children at such a young age. Several halachot indicate that Ashrei is one of the most significant prayers. One halacha states that if a person comes late to synagogue, he should skip over certain portions of the Pesukei d'Zimra, the Psalms of Praise, in order to catch up to the congregation. However, except in extreme circumstances, one should at least say Baruch she'Amar, Ashrei, and Yishtabach, indicating their importance.[1]

In the midst of Ashrei, there is a verse that states, פותח את ידך ומשביע לכל חי רצון, "You open Your hand and give sustenance to all living things." This passage is so vital that if you said it without focusing on its meaning, you must repeat this verse and onward, until the end of the psalm.[2] And finally, while we have an obligation to say the biblically mandated Shema twice daily, Ashrei is said *three* times a day, further stressing its value.

---

[1] *Code of Jewish Law*, OC 52:1.
[2] Ibid., OC 52:7, and the *Mishna Berura* there (16).

We've established that Ashrei is important, but the question remains: Why is this psalm elevated higher than all the other psalms we chant daily?

Thankfully, the Talmud itself asked the question:

כל האומר תהלה לדוד (תהלים קמה) בכל יום שלש פעמים, מובטח
לו שהוא בן העולם הבא.
מאי טעמא? אילימא משום דאתיא באל"ף בי"ת, נימא "אשרי
תמימי דרך" (תהלים קיט:א), דאתיא בתמניא אפין!
אלא משום דאית ביה "פותח את ידך" (תהלים קמה:טז). נימא
הלל הגדול, דכתיב ביה "נותן לחם לכל בשר" (תהלים קלו:כה)?
אלא משום דאית ביה תרתי. (ברכות ד:)

Anyone who says Tehilla l'David [Psalm 145] thrice
daily is promised to be a resident of the world to come.

Why? If you say that it is because it is arranged
in alphabetical order, then we [can just as easily] say
[Psalm 119], which does that eight times!

Rather, it is because it contains the verse "You
open Your hand [and give sustenance to all living
things]" (Tehillim 145:16). But then say the great
Hallel, which contains the verse "You give bread to
all living things" (Tehillim 136:25)?

Rather, it is because they contain both these things.
(Berachot 4b)

So as you can see, Ashrei has both – the acrostic and a special verse declaring G-d's responsibility to give sustenance to all. We can readily understand that a verse acknowledging G-d's bountiful sustenance is important. But why is the acrostic significant? Writing something in alphabetical order might have been a task we were assigned in grade school; why would an acrostic obligate us to recite Ashrei three times each day?

This question is sharpened when we consider the vast amount of biblical passages and *piyutim* that carry an acrostic – including most of Eicha, along with the vast amount of *kinot* said on Tisha b'Av, as well as the blessing preceding the Shema each morning, beginning א-ל ברוך גדול דעה and ending תמיד מספרים כבוד א-ל וקדושתו. On the holiest day of Yom Kippur, the *Vidui* (Confession) is also in the order of the Hebrew alphabet.

So, what's the big deal about the *alef-bet*?

Rav Soloveitchik once gave the following parable by way of explanation.[3] Let's assume you are praising the Almighty in public. You stand before the crowd and speak for over two hours, discussing the various attributes of G-d.

Finished? Have you now exhausted the topic? Have you comprehensively praised G-d?

Of course not! Unlike any other subject, it's impossible to ever exhaust the topic of G-d's greatness. It's no wonder that every Shabbat and holiday, as we recite the long Birkat Hashir,[4] starting with the words נשמת כל חי תברך את שמך, "Every living creature should praise Your name," and enumerating G-d's many praises, we say in its midst אין אנו מספיקים להודות לך, "We cannot praise You sufficiently." Despite the very long prayer, taking up at least two full pages in an average siddur, it is still inadequate.

Since there is no end to praising G-d, we limit ourselves to the *alef-bet*. The letters from *alef* to *taf* represent a *complete* unit (i.e., the entire Hebrew alphabet), within which we offer our attempts at praise. So too in the opposite case: on Tisha b'Av, when we commemorate the innumerable atrocities that the Jewish people were subject to, we limit our crying and our challenging of G-d to the *alef-bet*. And finally, on Yom Kippur, our sins and misgivings

---

[3] I heard this insight many years ago from Rabbi Jacob J. Schacter, in the name of the Rav. It can be found in print in a book published by Rabbi Schacter with the insights of the Rav on the Tisha b'Av kinot: *The Lord is Righteous in All His Ways* (Jersey City, NJ: Toras HoRav Foundation, Ktav, 2006), pages 134–136. See too *Koren Mesorat HaRav Kinot*, pages 298–299.

[4] Pesachim 118a.

through the year are numerous and too long to encompass properly. Thus, we limit ourselves to the Hebrew alphabet there as well.

Formulating ideas into words is a unique gift given to human beings over every other creature. And yet, despite the millions of written books, recorded lectures, and more, none of us can say that we've fully exhausted a given topic. Can anyone honestly say that they successfully told their husband, wife, or children how much they love them – with mere words?!

It should come as no surprise, therefore, that Ashrei concludes with the declaration, ואנחנו נברך י־ה מעתה ועד עולם הללויה, "We will praise Hashem, from now till forever!" Since we can never fully praise G-d we have limited ourselves to the *alef-bet*, yet this very structure leaves us with the feeling that there is so much more to be said...

Summary

As we recite Ashrei three times a day, let's remember our limitations of speech. Words alone can do justice in praising G-d properly, but not total justice. We therefore limit ourselves to the acrostic, and that limitation highlights the power of this prayer, the limitation of words, and the feeling that much more should be said to our spouses, our children, our friends, and of course to G-d.

The Global and the Particular: Reciting Shema with Its Blessings

שמע ישראל ה' אלוקינו ה' אחד (דברים ו:ד)

Hear, O Israel, G-d is our king, G-d is one. (Devarim 6:4)

Every morning and evening, the Jewish people recite this famous verse. It is probably one of the only biblical commandments we fulfill within our prayer service.[1] It is one of the first words taught to a Jewish child,[2] and one of the last a Jew says in this world.

---

[1] See the difference of opinion regarding whether the commandment is biblical in Berachot 21a: Rambam (*Sefer Hamitzvot*, positive commandment no. 10) claims that the obligation to recite Shema is of biblical origin, while the *Shita Mekubetzet* (Berachot 21a) claims that the verses in the Shema instructing us to "speak of these matters…when you go to bed and when you awaken" (Devarim 6:7) are referring to any Torah learning and not specifically to the words of the Shema.

[2] See Sukka 42a: תנו רבנן: קטן היודע לנענע – חייב בלולב. יודע לדבר – אביו לומדו תורה וקריאת שמע…קריאת שמע מאי היא? פסוק ראשון, "Our rabbis have taught: A young child who knows how the shake the four species [on Sukkot] is obligated in the mitzva of the four species…. If he knows how to speak, his father teaches him Torah and Shema…. What of Shema [should the child be taught]? The first verse."

But our sages didn't stop there; they decreed that we must surround Shema with blessings.[3] The two blessings that lead up to Shema, both in the morning and at night, prepare us for its recital. In order to better understand how we should approach Shema, let's take a closer look at these two blessings.

The first blessing (which begins with ברוך...יוצר אור ובורא חושך and ends with ברוך...יוצר המאורות) talks about the creation of the world. We bless G-d for creating light, the luminaries, and the entirety of nature. There is nothing specifically Jewish about this blessing; in relating to G-d as the creator of the world, this blessing bears a rather universal character.

The next blessing (beginning with אהבת עולם and ending with ברוך...הבוחר בעמו ישראל באהבה) talks about the love G-d has for the Jewish people. The blessing emphasizes devoting oneself to learning and upholding Torah values at all times, in return for G-d's eternal love for the Jewish people. Clearly, this blessing concerns itself with themes that are specifically Jewish.

With these two blessings – the first universal, the second Jewish – a Jew arrives at the Shema.

Fundamentally, this order should not surprise us, as this is the order that the Torah follows in Bereishit (Genesis). G-d created the entire world, and only then did He form a special relationship with Avraham and his offspring, the Jewish people. The Mishna follows the same order:

[רבי עקיבא] היה אומר: חביב אדם שנברא בצלם... חביבין ישראל שנקראו בנים למקום. (משנה אבות ג:יד)

[R. Akiva] would say: The human being is beloved, for he was created in His image.... The Jewish people, however, are beloved further, for they are called G-d's children. (Mishna Avot 3:14)

---

[3] Berachot 11a.

The Shema, with its accompanying blessings, expresses the multifaceted role of the Jewish people. On the one hand, we are part of the human race, benefiting, like all others from the stars and the moon, from the wonders of nature, and from G-d's creation.[4] But on the other hand, as the chosen people,[5] we share a unique relationship with G-d, which dictates a specific lifestyle. We therefore begin the blessings of the Shema with a global statement, to remind us of our responsibility to the world, and then we move on to focus particularly on the Jewish people. In so doing, we declare that *we have a responsibility both to the Jewish people as well as to the world at large*. In the words of Rav Soloveitchik:

> Famine, disease, war, oppression, materialism, atheism, permissiveness, pollution of the environment – all these are problems which history has imposed not only on the general community but also on the covenantal community. We have no right to tell mankind that these problems are exclusively theirs.

---

[4] Indeed, there are segments of the Jewish population who feel that there is nothing that one can learn from the world outside the confines of the Jewish community. On the other hand, support for the view that one *can* gain from the secular world can be found in endless places, such as the famous statement of the Midrash (Eicha Rabba 2:18): אם יאמר לך אדם יש חכמה בגוים – תאמן, "If someone says to you, 'There is wisdom among the non-Jews' – believe it!" Additionally, the Rambam writes that one can achieve the elevated level of "love of G-d through observing nature" (*Mishneh Torah, Hilchot Yesodei Hatorah* 2:2). Thus, one is required to recite a blessing ("Blessed...Who has bestowed wisdom on those who fear Him") when one sees a profound scholar of the Jewish people (Code of Jewish Law, OC 224:6), just as one is obligated to recite a blessing when one sees a non-Jewish scholar ("Blessed...Who has bestowed from His wisdom to the human race," ibid. 7).

[5] I thank a dear former congregant and close friend, Frank Medjuck of Halifax, for pointing out to me that rather than the Torah just being the Jews' genetic inheritance, the Jews "chose" to become the chosen nation when they "accepted" (having other choices) the proposal from G-d to become "a kingdom of priests and a holy nation" (Shemot 20).

(*Abraham's Journey: Reflections on the Life of the Founding Patriarch* [Jersey City, NJ: Ktav, 2008], page 203)

As believing Jews, we tend at times to conceive that our entire mission on earth is limited to the Jewish people only. We have been taught, time and again, to keep mitzvot, to learn Torah, and to raise our children in the way of the Torah. These challenges are far from easy, and the solutions are as complex as a knotted lace. Thus, one whole blessing crystallizes this point, using many adjectives to fully express its complexity.

But it doesn't stop there; we Jews also have a mission that extends across the entire globe. The Jewish message to all (Jews and Gentiles alike) is that one must abide by the seven Noahide commandments of ethical and upright moral behavior.[6] We Jews have to teach and preach it, and more importantly, be a living example of it – in our monetary dealings, in the way we speak to each other, and so much more.

Based on the source in Avot quoted above, it seems clear that as Jews we have more, not less, of a responsibility to live up to both our particular and universal obligations. If we are the "children" of G-d, then just like the older child helps raise the younger ones, we have a responsibility to help raise the other children of G-d, and transform this world into a more ethical and moral place. After all, in our ultimate trial before G-d after we leave this earth, we will not only be asked קבעת עיתים לתורה, "Did you [during the course of your life] set aside times to learn Torah," but also נשאת ונתת באמונה, "Did you conduct business in faith" being a living example of a child of G-d. Not only will G-d put us on the spot asking if ציפית לישועה, "Did you anxiously await the Redemption" that will foremost save the Jewish people, but also עסקת בפריה ורביה,

---

[6] *Mishneh Torah, Hilchot Melachim* 8:11.

"Did you produce offspring," ensuring the continuity of the world at large![7]

The famous Netziv of Volozhin, Rav Naftali Tzvi Yehuda Berlin, sees the greatness of our founding patriarchs as being both the above:

וזה היה שבח האבות, שמלבד שהיו צדיקים וחסידים ואוהבי ה'
באופן היותר אפשר, עוד היו ישרים, היינו שהתנהגו עם אומות
העולם, אפילו עובדי אלילים מכוערים, מכל מקום היו עמם
באהבה וחשו לטובתם באשר היא קיום הבריאה. (העמק דבר,
הקדמה לספר בראשית)

> And this was the greatness of the patriarchs, in that beyond being righteous, pious, and lovers of G-d to the utmost, they were honest – in other words they dealt with the nations, even the ugliest idolaters, with love, and they were concerned with their good, as that upholds creation. (*Haamek Davar*, introduction to Bereishit)

This duality came home when waiting once in line at passport control in Israel. After a rather long line, my turn finally arrived, and I greeted the lady behind the counter with a polite "Good afternoon, how are you holding up." She looked up and said, "You are the first person to actually wish me a good afternoon, and ask how I'm doing." Without batting an eyelash, I told her that she couldn't judge the others before me on line, as they were not religious Jews, or perhaps not even Jewish. However, she could and should hold someone like me to a higher standard. Unimpressed, she replied, "But Judaism just speaks about kosher food and Shabbat." I went on to quote various statements of our sages concerning interpersonal relationships and human conduct,

---

[7] See Shabbat 31a.

especially the dictate to say hello,[8] which are in the very same tractates as the laws she had referred to.

In a word, while the latter laws are the second paragraph of Shema, the former is a lesson that can be taught universally in the first paragraph of Shema.

Thus, looking at the Jewish state, one of the most amazing and miraculous achievements of all time, we must ask ourselves: Is modern-day Israel the living example of democracy, trumpeting a resounding message of morality and justice, as well as a place in which one lives and breathes Judaism?

Ultimately, this is the message that Chazal want us to remember every day. It's not just that "if we don't do mitzvot, it won't rain in Israel!" After all, we Jews read about the story of Adam and Eve, and Noach and the flood, each year just like we read about the events of the Jewish family, starting with Avraham and all the way through the generations. Rather, if we don't live up to our obligation of setting an example to the world, then the individual, the Jewish people, and the world at large will suffer as well. In the words of the Rambam:

> צריך כל אדם שיראה עצמו כל השנה כולה כאילו חציו זכאי וחציו חייב, וכן כל העולם חציו זכאי וחציו חייב. חטא חטא אחד הרי הכריע את עצמו **ואת כל העולם כולו** לכף חובה וגרם לו השחתה, עשה מצוה אחת הרי הכריע את עצמו **ואת כל העולם כולו** לכף זכות וגרם לו ולהם תשועה והצלה. (משנה תורה, הלכות תשובה ג:ד)

One should see oneself the entire year as if he is equal in his merits versus his sins, *as well as the entire world* being equal in merits and sins. If he did even one sin, he has tilted himself *and the entire world* to being

---

[8] Mishna Avot 4:15, Berachot 17a, regarding Rabban Yochanan ben Zakai always saying hello first – "even to the Gentile in the marketplace." See also part 1, "What Happened to the *Yasher Koach* Culture?"

liable and causing its destruction. If he does even one mitzva, then he tilted himself *and the entire world* to a positive verdict and brought salvation to himself and the world. (*Mishneh Torah, Hilchot Teshuva* 3:4)

There is a custom to touch your tefillin when you begin to say the first blessing of Shema.[9] At first glance, this seems a bit peculiar; you are touching your tefillin, a mitzva unique to the Jewish people, during a blessing discussing the entire universe! Rather, when we touch our tefillin, we are in essence saying that our unique relationship with G-d *creates an obligation toward the wider world.*

The message of these blessings is so vital that if you are late to shul in the morning, you must skip other parts of the service in order to have time to say them,[10] and you must recite them even at the expense of not catching up with the *chazan.*[11] Moreover, if you're unsure whether you've already said Shema, you must say it – together with the blessings preceding it.[12] Even though these blessings are only a rabbinic obligation (and in cases of doubt regarding rabbinic obligations we usually rule leniently),[13] the significance of these blessings demands that they be repeated.

Only after acknowledging our willingness to live up to our mission toward our fellow Jews, as well as to the world at large,

---

[9] For the sources of this custom, see *Yalkut Yosef*, 5764, Laws of the Psalms of Praise 59, footnote 2, page 461.

[10] *Code of Jewish Law*, OC 52:1.

[11] Ibid. 236:3.

[12] Ibid. 87:1. However, if a person is sure that he recited Shema and is only in doubt as to whether he said the blessings, he doesn't repeat the blessings (*Mishneh Torah, Hilchot Keriat Shema* 2:13). Moreover, the Code suggests that while one fulfills the biblical recitation of Shema if one said it without its blessings (and therefore one doesn't repeat the Shema with its blessings that were missed, but rather just the blessings), he recommends saying the blessings, as well as the Shema with them (OC 60:2).

[13] *Code of Jewish Law*, OC 174:4.

do we have a right (following the recitation of Shema) to mention G-d's everlasting promise to look out for the security of the Jewish people in the final blessings of Shema, immediately preceding the Amida. Appropriately enough, this blessing ends with the words גאל ישראל, "Who has redeemed Israel," in the morning, and שומר עמו ישראל לעד, "Who guards over Israel forever," at night.

Summary

We recite two blessings in order to prepare ourselves to accept the yoke of heaven with Shema: As G-d's children, daily declaring G-d's oneness, we are responsible both for ourselves, as well as for all of G-d's creations. We dare not be just a shining example for the former; rather we must also uphold our obligation to the latter.

Fast and Now: Foul Language

As part of my job, I find myself on airplanes more than the average member of my community. Though airport security has become quite an annoyance, what really bothers me about flying is seeing how people behave when they travel. Among the many negative traits, allow me to bring up but one: the *fast and now* syndrome. People push and shove to get on the plane first, even though we all know the plane won't leave without all its passengers once luggage has been checked in. So too, the cutting in line at passport control is extraordinary – after all, you usually have to wait for your luggage anyway. Finally, the impatience at the luggage conveyer is a sight to see....

Airport behavior is symptomatic of the world we live in – a world of fast foods and fast internet, when waiting even two minutes for something to "buffer" is already considered an unnecessary inconvenience. It can be "Peace Now," with no patience for working toward an enduring, safe peace, or even "Mashiach Now," for those who don't want to make the effort to bring the redemption but rather want it *right now*! The inability to work toward a goal has spawned a huge industry of "fast Judaism."

Each week, we Jews refrain from thirty-nine forbidden acts on Shabbat; these acts are almost all considered "creative acts," as they produce things that didn't exist previously.[1] And yet, one of these acts is none other than planting:

אבות מלאכות ארבעים חסר אחת: הזורע... (משנה שבת ז:ב)

The [forbidden] acts on Shabbat are forty less one: planting... (Mishna Shabbat 7:2)

What's the difference between planting and all the other prohibitions? The majority of the forbidden acts provide consequences immediately. You write on a piece of paper and can immediately read what you wrote. You cook a piece of meat and it's ready to be consumed an hour later. You plow a field and straightaway see the results. Only with planting do you have to wait months until you see results.[2] The long winter must pass before you can witness the fruits of your labor. And yet, this too is forbidden on Shabbat.

Each week, a Jew is taught to have patience, to value the process that brings about the end result. Just like it takes weeks of exercising and dieting to get into shape, so too it takes time to reach our goals.

This message appears in our tradition not only regarding Shabbat, but also in our prayers every morning and evening. In the second blessing preceding Shema, we reaffirm our commitment to work toward our goals and to invest the necessary time to achieve them:

אבינו האב הרחמן, המרחם, רחם עלינו, ותן בלבנו להבין ולהשכיל,
לשמוע, ללמוד וללמד, לשמור ולעשות, ולקיים את כל דברי תלמוד

---

[1] Such as writing a few letters on a piece of paper, sewing a shirt, etc. The only exception to this generalization is the prohibition of carrying on Shabbat in a place without an *eiruv*.

[2] There is a debate as to whether this is the case with cooking as well. See *Minchat Chinuch* 298, *Eglei Tal* 8, and *Aruch Hashulchan* 252.

תורתך באהבה. והאר עינינו בתורתך, ודבק לבנו במצוותיך. (אהבה
רבה, ברכה שנית של ברכות קריאת שמע, תפילת שחרית)

Our merciful Father, the compassionate one, have
mercy on us, enable our hearts to comprehend and
become wiser, to listen, learn, and teach, to observe
and to fulfill all of the Torah with love. And illuminate
our eyes with Your Torah, and allow us to cling to
Your mitzvot. (Ahava Rabba, the second blessing
before Shema in Shacharit)

And so too at night:

...בשכבנו ובקומנו נשיח בחוקיך ונשמח בדברי תורתך ובמצותיך
לעולם ועד, כי הם חיינו ואורך ימינו ובהם נהגה יומם ולילה.
(ברכה שנית של ברכות קריאת שמע, תפילת ערבית)

....When we go to sleep and when we wake up we
will talk of Your laws, and forever rejoice in Your
Torah and mitzvot, for they are our lifestyle and we
will study them day and night. (the second blessing
before Shema in Maariv)

Look how many verbs are used to express our devotion to work
toward the goal of learning and keeping the Torah: to comprehend,
become wiser, listen, learn, teach, observe, fulfill, illuminate,
cling. And then, summing it up concisely at night, "When we go
to sleep and when we wake up we will talk of Your laws, and
forever rejoice in Your Torah and mitzvot!"

It won't happen immediately. It will take time and effort, and
you may not see fruits right away. Indeed, one doesn't understand
the entirety of the Torah and the Jewish lifestyle overnight. Unlike
the "fast" world we function in, to achieve our goals we must
truly invest time and effort.

Years ago, I heard from my rebbe, Rav Rakeffet, an anecdotal story about a yeshiva student who was apprehended for speeding by a police officer. The officer asked the young student how long he'd been learning in the local yeshiva. When the student answered "eight years," the officer, rather taken aback, responded: "Eight years? You must be the dumbest student there. You've been there for eight years and you still haven't graduated?!"

I can literally fill a page with the number of rabbis who, when seen with an open *sefer* in front of them, were told by their congregants, "Why are you studying? I thought you graduated already!"

Indeed, the highest compliment one can pay to a Talmudic scholar is to brand him a תלמיד חכם, a wise student![3] One who is wise, in the realm of Judaism, is one who never stops being a "student," one who is always striving and knows that it's not a done deal in a short while.

The Torah never praised the fast and now, but rather the toil toward the end product:

שיר המעלות אשרי כל ירא ה' ההלך בדרכיו: **יגיע כפיך** כי תאכל אשריך וטוב לך: (תהלים קכח:א-ב)

A Song of Ascents. Happy is everyone who fears G-d, who walks in His ways. When you eat *the labor of your hands*, you shall be happy and it shall be well with you. (Tehillim 128:1–2)

---

[3] For the source of this term, see http://he.wikipedia.org/wiki/תלמיד_חכם

Summary

Every morning and evening, before accepting the yoke of heaven in Shema, a Jew declares firmly before G-d: "Though I live in the fast-and-now generation, I will fight to develop my trait of patience, to invest the time and effort needed in order to be a devoted soldier in G-d's army."

 **Part IV**

The Amida: A Daily
Audience with G-d

Hashem Sefatai Tiftach: An Innovative Addition and Nobody Screams "Reformer"?

We all know that in the Orthodox world, *the* cardinal sin is to change something. We pride ourselves on our tradition and consistency, with religious conduct that goes back generations. But there is a greater sin than changing, and that's adding. If you add to our tradition, in any way, you will be frowned upon and find yourself considered a reformer.[1]

And yet, the daily line that opens our Amida is, in fact, an addition! Following the establishment of the daily blessings of the Amida by the *Anshei Knesset Hagedola*, the Men of the Great Assembly,[2] and then Shmuel Hakatan's additional nineteenth blessing,[3] we would have thought that the text of the Amida

---

[1] The additions referred to above are not a violation of the biblical edict to refrain from adding or subtracting from the biblical commandments (Devarim 13:1), as the rabbis have a right to add additions to the Torah as they see fit (see Rashba, Rosh Hashana 16a) or add additional commandments that express an already existing commandment (Ramban, Devarim 4:2). In this case, when the Amida was sealed, we find an addition following it without anyone questioning if this constituted tampering with a sealed product.

[2] Megilla 17b.

[3] Berachot 29a.

would remain unchanged.[4] But alas, not only was an addition introduced, but amazingly, nobody seems to have questioned it:

> והא אמר רבי יוחנן: בתחלה אומר, "ה' שפתי תפתח" (תהלים
> נא:יז), ולבסוף הוא אומר, "יהיו לרצון אמרי פי" (תהלים יט:טו)?
> אלא, התם כיון דתקינו רבנן למימר "ה' שפתי תפתח", כתפלה
> אריכתא דמיא. (ברכות ד:)

> But didn't R. Yochanan say: At the beginning [of the Amida] one says, "G-d, open my lips" (Tehillim 51:17), and at the end one says, "May the words of my mouth…find favor" (Tehillim 19:15)? Rather, in that case, since the rabbis ordained to say "G-d, please open my lips," it is like a prolonged Amida prayer. (Berachot 4b)[5]

The Gemara here discusses two verses that were added to the Amida. The first verse, added to the beginning of the Amida, reads as follows: ה', שפתי תפתח ופי יגיד תהלתך, "G-d, please open my lips and let my mouth utter Your praises." The second verse, added to the end of the Amida, is: יהיו לרצון אמרי פי והגיון לבי לפניך ה', צורי וגואלי, "May the words of my mouth and the murmurings of my heart find favor before You, G-d, my rock and my redeemer." While the Gemara questions whether reciting the first verse constitutes a *hefsek*, an interruption between the concluding blessing of the Shema and the onset of the Amida, it does not

---

[4] Indeed, we usually don't tamper with these set blessings. See, for example, *Responsa Yechaveh Daat* by Rav Ovadya Yosef (OC 1:43) for the various sources indicating that we do not tamper with the blessings of the Men of the Great Assembly, since these sages combined great wisdom with the remnants of prophecy.

[5] The Men of the Great Assembly functioned for about two hundred years, from the end of the biblical era, while Rabbi Yochanan lived during the two generations of amoraim, many generations later (180–280 CE).

ask the basic question – why isn't the addition itself considered a problem?

One possible answer is to simply suggest that our generation is different from theirs. The line was added at a time in which rabbis had the power to fine-tune things. However, the Gemara does question other additions. For instance, just a few pages later, the Gemara asks why the latter addition, from Tehillim 19, was placed at the end of the Amida.[6] So we still must ask: Why is there no discussion about the addition of the verse ה' שפתי תפתח ופי יגיד תהלתך, "G-d, please open my lips and let my mouth utter Your praises"?

This leads me to believe that while the ending verse is a fine "addition," the former is *not* an addition, but rather *a declaration of the essence of prayer*! In other words, since this verse captures the fundamental undertone of the entire prayer service, there was never an issue made about its addition to the service.

Fundamentally, prayer is not an obligation to recite words, like the twice-daily obligation to *say* words of the Shema,[7] or the obligation to *read* the megilla on Purim.[8] Rather, prayer is the "service of the heart," it is an attempt to pour our hearts before G-d. And yet, now that prayer has been formalized, prayer is *all* about words! It is in order to soften this tension, and put the formalized text into perspective, we recite this opening verse, "G-d, please open my lips and let my mouth utter Your praises." It's vital that we *unite our lips with our hearts*, in genuine prayer before G-d.

---

[6] Berachot 9b.
[7] Ibid. 10b.
[8] Megilla 4a.

Summary

We begin the Amida with the verse, "G-d, please open my lips and let my mouth utter Your praises" (Tehillim 51:17). This verse expresses the essence of prayer: the desire to give form to what lies in our hearts. Since it's self-evident that this is the most appropriate way to begin the Amida, this addition isn't questioned. When the essence of prayer is added, there is no discussion!

"Welcome Back" after the Amida?

The late Rabbi Michael Katz, a former rosh yeshiva at Yeshiva University, approached a student following the silent Amida. He smiled, put out his hand to shake that of his student, and said loudly, "*Shalom aleichem* and welcome back."

The student, rather bewildered and surprised, responded to his teacher, "But Rebbe, I didn't go anywhere. I just finished the Amida."

Without batting an eyelash, Rabbi Katz responded to his confused student by saying, "Not at all – during the Amida you were thinking of your test this morning, of where you're taking your girlfriend this Saturday night, the baseball game on TV last night… Now, once the Amida is over, you've returned to this room. So, I politely offered a warm *Shalom aleichem* upon your return!"[1]

How many of us can relate to that student during the Amida? It seems that when we are alone with G-d, a G-d we don't physically see, it's rather hard, to say the least, to concentrate for the entire duration of the experience, without our head diverging to areas far and beyond the words of the siddur!

---

[1] Heard from Rav Aharon Rakeffet.

It's almost impossible, in an age in which the attention span is so low, to concentrate for many minutes on the words and to be mentally present. And yet, the Amida experience is not meant to be the "work of the lips" but rather that of the heart. Moreover, it's far more than just opening your heart to anyone, but rather…

המתפלל צריך שיראה עצמו **כאילו שכינה כנגדו**. (סנהדרין כב.)

One who is praying [the Amida] must see himself *as if the holy presence of G-d is right in front of him.* (Sanhedrin 22a)

G-d is right there, in front of my nose, and I, a lowly Jew, actually have a private audience with G-d!

But my mind will drift! Even if I start by taking the three steps backward and forward, indicating that I am entering into a lofty and private audience with G-d,[2] how can I possibly be expected to concentrate for the entire duration of the Amida? It's impossible to do ad hoc!

Perhaps this is the reason why our sages dictated the following idea:

ישהה שעה אחת קודם שיקום להתפלל, כדי שיכוין לבו למקום. (שולחן ערוך, אורח חיים צג:א)

One should devote one hour [for meditation] before praying [the Amida] in order to direct one's heart to G-d. (*Code of Jewish Law*, OC 93:1, based on Berachot 30b)

An hour before the Amida? Who has the time? Perhaps this is the reason why the *Mishna Berura* minimizes it a bit:

---

[2] See *Mishneh Torah, Hilchot Tefilla u'Nesiat Kapayim* 5:10–11 and *Aruch Hashulchan*, OC 123:1.

ומיהו זה לחסידים, ולשאר עם די בשעה מועטת שישהא קודם
שיתחיל שהוא כדי הילוך ח' טפחים. (משנה ברורה צג:א)

This was for the [special] pious ones but for the masses
it's sufficient to wait a "small hour" before praying,
which is equivalent to walking eight handbreadths.
(*Mishna Berura* 93:1)

The time is less…but the idea is the same; in order for us to open our
hearts and concentrate properly throughout the service, we need a
few minutes of "time-out," in which we shut out all distractions in
order to stand in front of G-d without being sidetracked.[3]

It's far from being easy! I would venture that the majority of
Jews…*usually can't concentrate properly.*

The good news is that we're not alone. Even the great rabbis of
the Talmud had the problem:

א"ר חייא רובא: אנא מן יומיי לא כיונית אלא חד זמן... א"ר מתניה:
אנא מחזק טיבו לראשי, דכד הוה מטי מודים הוא כרע מגרמיה...
(ירושלמי, ברכות ב:ד)

Said R. Chiya Ruba: All my days, I didn't concentrate
[during prayers] except once…. Said R. Matanya: I
have a head that automatically bows down when I
utter the words *modim*… (Yerushalmi, Berachot 2:4)

While understanding the words is only critical for the first
blessing,[4] the feeling of standing before G-d must be there for the
entirety of the service. In the words of the Rambam:

---

[3] This is the reason why one should relieve oneself before praying, and failure
to do so is no less than an "abomination" before G-d (*Code of Jewish Law*,
OC 92:1).

[4] Failure to understand the first blessing nullifies the prayer – see *Code of
Jewish Law*, OC 101:1. See also the words of the *Mishna Berura* (OC 60:7),
who makes a distinction between the intent to fulfill an obligation by virtue
of a particular action about to be done, versus intent that you are doing a

ה דברים מעכבין את התפלה...וכוונת הלב... כיצד? כל תפלה שאינה
בכוונה אינה תפילה, ואם התפלל בלא כוונה חוזר ומתפלל בכוונה.
מצא דעתו משובשת ולבו טרוד, אסור לו להתפלל עד שתתישב
דעתו. (משנה תורה, הלכות תפילה ונשיאת כפיים ד:א)

Five things invalidate prayer...and the intent of the
heart.... How so? Any prayer that is without *kavana*
is not a prayer, and if one prays without intent one
must return and pray again. If one's mind is very
preoccupied and one's heart is very disturbed, it's
forbidden to pray until one's mind is settled. (*Mishneh
Torah, Hilchot Tefilla u'Nesiat Kapayim* 4:1)

As Reb Chaim "Brisker" Solovetchik (the famed grandfather of
the more contemporary Rav Soloveitchik) stated in his interpretation to the Rambam's Code:

...ונראה דכוונה זו אינה מדין כוונה, רק שהוא **מעצם מעשה
התפלה**, ואם אין לבו פנוי, ואינו רואה את עצמו שעומד לפני
ד' ומתפלל, אין זה מעשה תפלה. (חידושי רבינו חיים הלוי על
הרמב"ם, עמוד 6)

...and it seems that this "intent" is not identical to
the intent [required in other realms of Halacha], but
rather *it's part and parcel of the action of prayer*, and
if one's heart is not open and one doesn't see oneself
as standing before G-d and praying, this is not prayer
at all! (*The Insights of Rabbeinu Chaim HaLevi on
the Rambam*, page 6)

---

mitzva and not something else, i.e., when standing before G-d in prayer one
should have intent to speak to G-d, and not just to bow and move to and fro.

Summary

Don't jump into the Amida! Take a few seconds, and try to clear your head and create a prayer, rather than a four-minute lip service. Easy it's not, vital it is. We want to *pray*, after all!

Praise: G-d Needs a Mortal to Praise Him?

דרש רבי שמלאי: לעולם יסדר אדם שבחו של הקב"ה ואחר כך
יתפלל. מנלן? ממשה, דכתיב "ואתחנן אל ה' בעת ההיא", וכתיב
"ה' אלקים אתה החלת להראות את עבדך את גדלך ואת ידך החזקה
אשר מי אל בשמים ובארץ אשר יעשה כמעשיך וכגבורותיך", וכתיב
בתריה "אעברה נא ואראה את הארץ הטובה וגו'" (דברים ג:כג–
כה). (ברכות לב.)

Deduced R. Simlai: One should always bring praise
[before G-d] first, and then "pray" [request]. From
where do we learn this law? From Moshe, as it says,
"I beseeched the Lord at that time," and then it says,
"O Lord, G-d, You have begun to show Your servant
Your greatness and Your strong hand, for who is like
God in heavens or on earth who can do as Your actions
and Your might?" and only then it says, "Let me cross
over and see the good land..." (Devarim 3:23–25).
(Berachot 32a)

Our Amida begins with three Blessings of Praise to G-d, showing
His greatness and might, and especially His unlimited power. We
mention that G-d is "the great, mighty, and awesome... [Who]
resurrects the dead...possesses the power to save...sustains the
living with kindness" and so much more.

Saying these words three times a day, following the above edict of our sages, one begins to wonder: Does G-d need my praise? I can understand that one can "butter up" a fellow human being prior to requesting something of him, but would we fathom, even for a moment, that this would be the case when speaking to the Almighty? Moreover, can any mortal Jew truly leave the Amida thinking, "G-d feels so much better now, with His self-image far higher, because *I* praised him?"

I personally believe that the above is one of the most primitive notions one can have of G-d. Therefore, the sages' edict has to be seen in context of its source text above, namely, Moshe's prayer that G-d overrule His own decree that Moshe not be allowed into the Holy Land. In his prayer, Moshe mentions G-d's great power, and only then petitions G-d to change the decree forbidding him from entering Israel. This equation is, I believe, the proper interpretation to the above law; if we want to ask things of G-d, *we have to first acknowledge who G-d is*, and only then does it make sense to petition G-d for whatever is on our agenda. Without acknowledging G-d's might, it doesn't make sense to petition Him.

This three-times-a-day exercise disciplines a Jew to one of the most fundamental lessons of life: we don't worship ourselves, or any other human being. We will only worship something far and beyond us, namely, G-d. No human, as big, rich, famous, and successful as he or she may be, will live forever. Thus, we will only worship and bow before G-d, not ourselves.

If this lesson is internalized thrice daily, perhaps it would allow us to exit the service and return to life with a different, more balanced perspective: let us not take ourselves too seriously. If we do, we run the risk of thinking that any foible or disappointment is no less than a conspiracy against the Jewish people! However, if one trains oneself to constantly praise G-d, and thus put the human being (ourselves included) in the proper proportional perspective,

I believe we will be able to deal with various disappointments in a more balanced fashion.

My rebbe, Rav Amital, would say each year around Purim time: "One who doesn't have a sense of humor doesn't have proper *yirat Shamayim* (awe of Heaven)!"[1] This statement challenges us to laugh at ourselves a bit, and thus have a balanced perspective as to who we are, versus the Almighty G-d. If we do have this healthy perspective, we will be able to make the proper distinction between a real problem versus a small one, a slight slip of the tongue versus a true insult, and an accident versus a conspiracy.

Once we have this perspective, of praising G-d on the one hand, and not over-praising oneself on the other, we will allow small misfortunes, be it wrong change at the store, not getting the *aliya* in synagogue on a day that you're commemorating a yartzeit, or someone tripping you, to go by without making a major issue. If we don't over-praise ourselves, but do over-praise G-d, I believe we will be a bit less sensitive to every petty word thrown our way. In the words of the Talmud:

כל המעביר על מדותיו מעבירין לו על כל פשעיו, שנאמר "נשא עון ועבר על פשע" (מיכה ז:יח) - למי "נושא עון"? למי שעובר על פשע. (ראש השנה יז.)

> Whoever lets things "slide" a bit, G-d will also let his sins "slide," as it says, "He allows the sin to slide, and passes over the transgression" (Micha 7:18). For whom does G-d let the "sin slide"? For those who

---

[1] I would add that this might explain why our sages, when describing G-d's daily schedule, insisted that among other things, G-d spends time each day "playing with the *livyatan* fish" (Avoda Zara 3b)! As these statements are meant for us to "imitate G-d," as you will, fulfilling the edict of והלכת בדרכיו, "and you shall follow in the ways of G-d" (Shabbat 133b, Sota 14a), it seems clear that our sages are instructing us to "play" a bit, to not take every little aspect of life with complete seriousness. After all, even G-d Almighty, as you will, "plays" a bit each day!

themselves slide over transgressions done to them. (Rosh Hashana 17a)

While we all possess a divine image, and while the psalmist states that the human being is "just a bit smaller then G-d,"[2] we are also just "dust from the earth."[3] At times we can sink very low, to the extent that the psalmist continues the very same psalm with "What is the human that I should even mention him!"

With these praises to G-d alone, one can approach life in a far more balanced way, knowing one's place in the world.

Summary

We don't praise G-d in order to extend pleasantries prior to asking for what we want. Rather, praise is an integral part of prayer, as without acknowledging the greatness and ability of G-d, one would not petition G-d. Moreover, by praising G-d rather than ourselves, we can gain a proper perspective on life, understanding that we shouldn't take ourselves too seriously given that only G-d Almighty is worthy of all the praises.

---

[2] Tehillim 8:6. See also Berachot 10a, where the Gemara parallels the human soul with no less than…G-d!

[3] Bereishit 2:7.

Lemaan Shemo: Do Me a Favor – for You?

We all ask for favors once in a while. There are always times when we need a bit of help to get by. But have you ever asked for a favor by saying, "Lend me a hundred dollars *for your sake*"? Clearly, that would be an illogical request – you're asking for the money for your *own* sake. And yet, we do exactly that thrice daily in the very first blessing of the Amida:

...ומביא גואל לבני בניהם למען שמו באהבה.

...He lovingly brings a redeemer to their children's children, for the sake of His name.

G-d brings redemption – *for G-d's sake*? Not for our sake? In what way is bringing redemption for G-d's sake?

The idea of G-d saving us for His sake doesn't only come up in our prayers; it's actually an old "trick" used throughout the Bible. King Shlomo mentions it when offering a prayer to G-d at the Temple's dedication:

וגם אל הנכרי אשר לא מעמך ישראל הוא ובא מארץ רחוקה למען שמך: (מלכים א, ח:לט-מא)

And also to the stranger, who is not of Your people Israel, but comes from a distant country for the sake of Your name... (I Melachim 8:39–41)

And Yirmiyahu uses it to beseech G-d's forgiveness for the people:

אם עוונינו ענו בנו ה' עשה למען שמך כי רבו משובתינו לך חטאנו:
(ירמיהו יד:ז)

If our iniquities have testified against us, O Lord, act for
Your name's sake, for our backslidings have increased;
we have sinned against You. (Yirmiyahu 14:7)

In Tehillim, too, this idea crops up:

למען שמך ה' וסלחת לעוני כי רב הוא: (תהלים כה:יא)

For Your name's sake, O Lord, forgive my iniquity,
for it is great. (Tehillim 25:11)

This last verse is the most difficult – G-d shall forgive our many
sins for *G-d's* sake?

It seems that there's a common thread in all of the above: G-d
took a chance with the Jews, and intertwined His name with ours.
As the verse states,

וראו כל עמי הארץ כי שם ה' נקרא עליך ויראו ממך: (דברים כח:י)

Then all the peoples of the earth will see that the name
of the Lord is called upon you, and they will fear you.
(Devarim 28:10)

This twenty-eighth chapter of Devarim details the blessings that
will be showered upon the Jewish people if we observe G-d's
Torah, and the punishments that will befall us if we fail to keep
G-d's Torah. In the midst of describing these blessings, G-d
envisions our ideal state: we fulfill our mission to such an extent
that the nations see the Jewish people as reflecting G-d's values.
Then it will be clear to all that G-d aligns His name with us.[1]

---

[1] For this reason the sages suggested that this verse alludes to the tefillin we

The end of u'Netaneh Tokef, the frightening prayer chanted in the Ashkenazic liturgy on the High Holidays, similarly expresses this idea:

שמך נאה לך, ואתה נאה לשמך, **ושמנו קראת בשמך.** עשה למען שמך, וקדש את שמך על מקדישי שמך.

Your name is worthy of You, and You are worthy of Your name, and *our name has been called in Your name.* Act for the sake of Your name, and sanctify Your name by those who sanctify it.

No less than we, flesh-and-blood Jews, have been called in G-d's name! It follows that if we act in an upright manner, we elevate the name of G-d. If we sink, however, to become degraded villains, then heaven forbid, we bring G-d's name down with us. As defined clearly by our sages:[2]

היכי דמי חילול השם? אמר רב: כגון אנא. אי שקילנא בישרא מטבחא ולא יהיבנא דמי לאלתר...

יצחק דבי רבי ינאי אמר: כל שחביריו מתביישין מחמת שמועתו (היינו חילול השם)...

כדתניא, "ואהבת את ה' אלקיך" (דברים ו:ה) – שיהא שם שמים מתאהב על ידך, שיהא קורא ושונה ומשמש תלמידי חכמים, ויהא משאו ומתנו בנחת עם הבריות. מה הבריות אומרות עליו? אשרי אביו שלמדו תורה, אשרי רבו שלמדו תורה. אוי להם לבריות שלא למדו תורה, פלוני שלמדו תורה ראו כמה נאים דרכיו כמה מתוקנים מעשיו. עליו הכתוב אומר, "ויאמר לי עבדי אתה ישראל אשר בך אתפאר" (ישעיהו מט:ג).

אבל מי שקורא ושונה ומשמש תלמידי חכמים ואין משאו ומתנו באמונה ואין דבורו בנחת עם הבריות, מה הבריות אומרות

---

wear on our heads: when wearing the tefillin, the name of G-d (within the paragraphs written on the parchments of the tefillin) is physically on our heads (Berachot 6a).

[2] Yoma 86a.

עליו? אוי לו לפלוני שלמד תורה, אוי לו לאביו שלמדו תורה,
אוי לו לרבו שלמדו תורה. פלוני שלמד תורה ראו כמה מקולקלין
מעשיו וכמה מכוערין דרכיו. ועליו הכתוב אומר, "באמור להם עם
ה' אלה ומארצו יצאו" (יחזקאל לו:כ).

What constitutes profanation of the Name? Rav said: If I take meat from the butcher and do not pay him immediately....

Yitzchak, of the school of R. Yannai, said: If one's colleagues are ashamed of his reputation, that constitutes a profanation of the Name....

Abaye explained: As it was taught: "And you shall love the Lord your G-d" (Devarim 6:5) – i.e., that the name of Heaven be beloved because of you. If someone studies Tanach and Mishnah, and attends on the disciples of the wise, is honest in business, and speaks pleasantly to others, what do people then say concerning him? "Happy the father who taught him Torah, happy the teacher who taught him Torah. Woe to people who have not studied the Torah, for this man who has studied the Torah – look how fine his ways are, how righteous his deeds!" Of him does Scripture state, "And He said to me: You are My servant, Israel, *in whom I will be glorified.*"

But if someone studies Tanach and Mishnah, attends to the disciples of the wise, but is dishonest in business, and not courteous in his relations with people, what do people say about him? "Woe to he who studied the Torah, woe to his father who taught him Torah, woe to his teacher who taught him Torah! This man studied the Torah – look how corrupt are his deeds, how ugly his ways." Of him Scripture says, "In that men said of them: These are the people *of the Lord*, and they are gone forth from His land."

So when we say למען שמו, "for the sake of His name," we are not trying to trick G-d. Rather, this was G-d's original plan when He entered into a partnership with the Jewish people. Like any two partners, if one is messing up the business, the other suffers as well.

But why would G-d do this? After all, the number of religious Jews filling jail sentences today is painful and frightening to consider. We've messed up endless times, from the sin of the golden calf to just yesterday. Why would G-d form a partnership with a partner who was doomed to fail?

To answer this we must return to Devarim chapter 28, this time to the verse just before the one previously quoted:

> יקימך ה' לו לעם קדוש כאשר נשבע לך כי תשמר את מצות ה'
> אלקיך **והלכת בדרכיו**. (דברים כח:ט)

> The Lord will establish you as His holy people as He swore to you, if you observe the commandments of the Lord, your G-d, and *walk in His ways*. (Devarim 28:9)

G-d commands us to "walk in His ways" – namely, to imitate G-d in the ways He runs the world. As our sages teach:

> מאי דכתיב, "אחרי ה' אלקיכם תלכו" (דברים יג:ה)? וכי אפשר לו
> לאדם להלך אחר שכינה? ...אלא להלך אחר מדותיו של הקב"ה.
> מה הוא מלביש ערומים..., אף אתה הלבש ערומים. הקב"ה ביקר
> חולים..., אף אתה בקר חולים.... הקב"ה ניחם אבלים..., אף אתה נחם
> אבלים. הקב"ה קבר מתים..., אף אתה קבור מתים. (סוטה יד.)

> What does it mean when it says, "After the Lord your G-d you shall follow" (Devarim 13:5)? Is it possible for a human being to walk after G-d? ...Rather it means to follow in the behavior of G-d: just like G-d clothes the naked...so too you; just like G-d visits the

sick…so too you; G-d comforted the bereaved…so too you; G-d buried the dead…so too you. (Sota 14a)

Who will influence another human being to be merciful? Who will teach them to visit the sick, and provide burial for the dead, if not the Jewish people, who have been taught this attribute so well? We were charged with the task of rectifying the world, and in preparation for this role we have been learning the word of G-d through G-d's Torah since our inception as a nation. It's up to us to bring G-d's name into this world. For this reason G-d entered into a partnership with us, despite the fact that we would mess up.

As I heard endless times from my rebbe, Rav Amital, when a Jew dies, G-d's name is diminished in the world. Our reaction is therefore to recite Kaddish, declaring, יתגדל ויתקדש שמיה רבה, "May His great name [yet, despite the current situation] be magnified and sanctified!" When such a radical occurrence happens, we have to go to the opposite end of the spectrum. In the words of the prophet:

ואחמל **על שם קדשי** אשר חללהו בית ישראל בגוים אשר באו שמה: לכן אמר לבית ישראל כה אמר אדנ-י ה' **לא למענכם אני עשה** בית ישראל **כי אם לשם קדשי** אשר חללתם בגוים אשר באתם שם: וקדשתי את שמי הגדול המחלל בגוים אשר חללתם בתוכם וידעו הגוים כי אני ה' נאם אדנ-י ה' בהקדשי בכם לעיניהם: ולקחתי אתכם מן הגוים וקבצתי אתכם מכל הארצות והבאתי אתכם אל אדמתכם: ...ואת רוחי אתן בקרבכם... (יחזקאל לו:כא-כז)

But I had pity on *My holy Name*, which the house of Israel had profaned among the nations to which they had come. Therefore, say to the house of Israel: "So says the Lord G-d: *Not for your sake do I do this,* O house of Israel*, but for My holy Name*, which you have profaned among the nations to which they have come. And I will sanctify *My great Name*, which was profaned among the nations, which you have

profaned in their midst; and the nations shall know
that I am the Lord, declares the Lord G-d, when I will
be sanctified through you before their eyes. *For I will
take you from among the nations and gather you from
all the countries, and I will bring you to your land....*
And I will put My spirit within you.... (Yechezkel
36:21–27)

As you can see, the prophet was told by the G-d that the way in
which G-d's holy name will once again be sanctified is *through
helping the Jewish people!* Even though G-d makes clear that this
will be done "*Not for your sake do I do this,* O house of Israel, *but
for My Holy Name,*" the method is through bringing the *Jewish
people* back to the Land of Israel.

Our sages express this idea beautifully when they discuss
what's written in the tefillin of G-d:

אמר ליה רב נחמן בר יצחק לרב חייא בר אבין: הני תפילין דמרי
עלמא מה כתיב בהו?
אמר ליה: "ומי כעמך ישראל גוי אחד בארץ וכו'" (דברי הימים
א, יז:כא). אמר להם הקדוש ברוך הוא לישראל: "אתם עשיתוני
חטיבה אחת בעולם, ואני אעשה אתכם חטיבה אחת בעולם."
(ברכות ו:)

Said R. Nachman ben Yitzchak to R. Chiya ben Avin:
The tefillin of the Master of the Universe – what's
written in them?

He answered: "Who is like Your nation, Israel, a
unique nation on earth..." (I Divrei Hayamim 17:21).
Said G-d to the Jewish people: "You made Me one
in the world, and I will make you one in the world!"
(Berachot 6b)

Summary

Do it for us because we represent You. We're in it together.

Do it for You! We're partners.

"Near," "No, Far," Say the Two-Headed Monsters: The First Two Blessings of the Amida and Kedusha

One of the "joys" of fatherhood is the unwritten obligation to watch TV with my kids. On one such occasion, I was sitting in front of the TV together with them, and looking uninterestedly at a *Sesame Street* program featuring the two-headed monsters, a character consisting of one body with two heads. They were manning the camera, and as was their "custom" since my own childhood, they were arguing with one another.

The argument revolved around the camcorder that was filming the show; one of the two heads insisted that the camera film from a distance while the other was adamant that the show be filmed as a close-up. Or in their words, "Near," "No, far," "Not far – near," "far," "near," "far"… As you can imagine, the picture was going in and out, becoming large and then small, making an impatient father rather dizzy.

As this went on for what seemed like quite a while, it hit me that we echo that very argument every day. When praying with a minyan, we recite Kedusha during the *chazan*'s repetition of the Amida. In it, we attempt to praise G-d like the angels do, as we state at the beginning of Kedusha: נקדש את שמך בעולם כשם שמקדישים אותו בשמי מרום, "Let us sanctify Your name in the world, as they do above."[1] Standing erect with our feet together,[2] just as the angels do above,[3] the congregation engages in a dialogue with the *chazan*:

חזן. ...״וקרא זה אל זה ואמר״:

קהל. ״קדוש קדוש קדוש ה׳ צבאות מלא כל הארץ כבודו״ (ישעיהו ו:ג).

חזן. לעומתם ברוך יאמרו (משבחים ואומרים):

קהל. ״ברוך כבוד ה׳ ממקומו״ (יחזקאל ג:יב).

חזן. ובדברי קדשך כתוב לאמר:

קהל. ״ימלוך ה׳ לעולם אלוקיך ציון לדור ודור הללוי-ה״ (תהלים קמו:י).

CHAZAN. "And they call to each other and say":

CONGREGATION. "Holy, holy, holy is the Lord of Hosts; the entire universe is full of His glory" (Yeshayahu 6:13).

CHAZAN. In response to them, they bless and say:

CONGREGATION. "Blessed is the glory of G-d from His place" (Yechezkel 3:12).

CHAZAN. And in Your holy writings it states:

---

[1] This is the Ashkenazic phrasing. The Sephardic tradition expresses the same idea in different words: נקדישך ונעריצך כסוד שיח שרפי קודש המשלשים לך קדושה, "Let us sanctify and admire, as the secret murmurings of the holy angels above express Your holiness."

[2] *Code of Jewish Law*, OC 95:4.

[3] Berachot 10b.

CONGREGATION. "G-d will rule forever, the Lord of Zion, for generation to generation, *halleluya*" (Tehillim 146:10).

We recite these words regularly, yet they actually contain an outright contradiction:

קדוש, קדוש, קדוש ה' צבאות, מלא כל הארץ כבודו.	ברוך כבוד ה' ממקומו.
Holy, holy, holy is the Lord of Hosts; *the entire universe* is full of His glory.	Blessed is the glory of G-d from *His place*.

Well, which is it? Is G-d's glory so enormous that it fills the entire world? Or is it limited to "His place," somewhere on high?

The answer, of course, is that both are correct. G-d is near and G-d is far, all at the same time. G-d's glory is everywhere, yet it is also very far from us. Indeed, the first phrase was originally said by the prophet Yeshayahu, who served as a prophet in Israel during the First Temple, when one could vividly feel G-d's presence in the land in which "constantly, the eyes of the Lord your G-d are on it from the onset of the year till its end" (Devarim 11:12). Therefore, it's no wonder that the established custom is to rise up a bit when we say these words, as they symbolize closeness to G-d, and we, as it were, are trying to get closer to Him.[4] The second clause was uttered by the prophet Yechezkel, who prophesied in the darkness of the Babylonian exile. He could therefore only long for G-d "from G-d's place," a place far from the alien soil upon which he stood. Our sages hinted at this when they contrasted the two:

---

[4] *Magen Avraham*, OC 125:2.

כָּל שֶׁרָאָה יְחֶזְקֵאל רָאָה יְשַׁעְיָה. לְמָה יְחֶזְקֵאל דּוֹמֶה? לְבֶן כְּפָר שֶׁרָאָה
אֶת הַמֶּלֶךְ. וּלְמָה יְשַׁעְיָה דּוֹמֶה? לְבֶן כְּרַךְ שֶׁרָאָה אֶת הַמֶּלֶךְ. (חגיגה
יג:)

Everything that Yechezkel saw, Yeshayahu saw as
well. To what can Yechezkel be compared? To a
villager who saw the king. To what can Yeshayahu
be compared? To a city dweller who saw the king.
(Chagiga 13b)[5]

The Talmud establishes that both prophets saw the same image of
G-d, but while Yechezkel was amazed by it, Yeshayahu was not,
since he had the privilege of feeling G-d's presence in the Holy
Land every day. It's like a newcomer to the city who first sees
the skyscrapers of NYC, versus the resident of Manhattan; while
the former is fascinated by the sight, the latter has seen it many a
time. It is not, therefore, that G-d changed, but rather that the two
prophets perceived G-d differently due to the different situations
and environments in which they saw the image of G-d.

When one is comforting a mourner, at a time when G-d's
presence seems far away, one customarily says **הַמָּקוֹם יְנַחֵם אוֹתְךָ**
בְּתוֹךְ שְׁאָר אֲבֵלֵי צִיּוֹן וִירוּשָׁלַיִם, "May the *place of G-d* comfort you
together with all mourners of Zion and Jerusalem." Similarly,
after reading from the Torah on Mondays or Thursdays, when
beseeching G-d to redeem the Jewish people from various harsh
predicaments they are in, we again invoke this description of G-d
as we pray:

אַחֵינוּ כָּל בֵּית יִשְׂרָאֵל הַנְּתוּנִים בְּצָרָה וּבַשִּׁבְיָה הָעוֹמְדִים בֵּין בַּיָּם
וּבֵין בַּיַּבָּשָׁה **הַמָּקוֹם** יְרַחֵם עֲלֵיהֶם וְיוֹצִיאֵם מִצָּרָה לִרְוָחָה...

---

[5] The Talmud is trying to understand the discrepancy between the length of
their prophecies. Yechezkel, in the famous מעשה המרכבה (description of G-d's
chariot) elaborated on his description of seeing the image of G-d (Yechezkel
1:4–28, a total of twenty-four verses). Yeshayahu, on the other hand, devoted
just a few words to the topic (Yeshayahu 6:2–4).

Our brothers, the house of Israel, who are in trouble
and in captivity, be it on land or sea, may the *place of
G-d* have mercy on them and remove them from their
sorrow to abundance....

And in the Shabbat and holiday morning prayers, during the
prolonged Kedusha, we too emphasize this. Right after uttering
ברוך כבוד ה' ממקומו, "Blessed is the Glory of G-d from His place,"
we state:

ממקומך מלכנו תופיע ותמלוך עלינו כי מחכים אנחנו לך. מתי
תמלוך בציון...

From your place, our King, please come and rule over
us, as we are waiting for You. When will You [again]
reign over Zion...

When there is trouble, and G-d's presence feels distant, we use
the term המקום, "the place" that is far from us. But when G-d
feels near, we experience G-d as filling the universe. Therefore,
Kedusha opens with this vision: נקדש את שמך בעולם כשם שמקדישים
אותו בשמי מרום, "Let us sanctify Your name in the world, as they
do above." If we sanctify the world down here as the angels do
above, then indeed G-d's glory will fill it all.

As Rabbi Shimon Schwab suggests, this may be one of the
reasons why Jews customarily *shokel* (sway back and forth)
during the prayer service:[6] swaying forward shows the Jew's
desire to draw closer to G-d, experiencing G-d as a close and
loving parent, while swaying backward expresses the realization
that, after all, G-d is far from us.[7]

---

[6] *Code of Jewish Law*, Rama's glosses, OC 48:1.

[7] "Ashrei," in *Rabbi Shimon Schwab on Prayer: The Great Rav's Teachings
on the Siddur* (ArtScroll Mesorah Publications, 2001), page 167.

It's no wonder that we can refer to G-d in our prayers as both אבינו, "our Father," as well as מלכנו, "our King," in the very same sentence.[8]

This tension between experiencing G-d as imminent versus transcendent – near yet far – is evident throughout our tradition, beyond the realm of the prayer service. Each time you take a sandwich in your hands, you express this same idea:

ברוך אתה ה', אלוקינו מלך העולם, המוציא לחם מן הארץ.

Blessed are You, G-d, our Lord, King of the universe,
Who brings forth bread from the ground.

In one short blessing, we move from addressing G-d in the second person, ("Blessed are *You*, G-d,") to the third person, ("Who brings forth bread"). Why switch midsentence?

The answer is that this is how a Jew goes through life – sometimes G-d is near and sometimes far, sometimes you feel that G-d is tapping you on the shoulder, and sometimes G-d seems to have abandoned you. In times of hardship, you may feel that G-d's glory is limited to a "place," while at other times G-d's presence may seem so close that it fills the entire world.

ובכל הברכות והתפלות אנו מדברים אליו יתברך בלשון נוכח, "ברוך אתה", ובמזמורים והודאות יש כמה שאומרים "אתה הוא" – נוכח ונסתר? והענין מובן. כי עצמותו יתברך נעלם מכל נעלם...ורק על-ידי מעשיו ניכר לנו... ולכן בתפלות שאנו מבקשים ממנו יתברך שיעשה כך וכך הלא מדברים מצד פעולותיו, ולכן אומרים "אתה". וכן בכל מיני ברכות ברכות כמו ברכת הנהנין שאנו מברכין על שברא פירא זו או לחם זה הלא מדברים בפעולותיו. (ערוך השולחן, הלכות יסודי הדת והשכמת הבוקר ה:ב)

---

[8] In the fourth blessing of the Grace after Meals (*Code of Jewish Law*, OC 188:1), between Rosh Hashana and Yom Kippur (ibid., 584:1, 601:1), and on most fast days.

In all the blessings, we speak to the Lord, blessed be He, in the first person, [saying,] "Blessed are You," but in the psalms of praise and thanksgiving we use both first and third person? But the matter is clear. For His essence is entirely hidden…and we can recognize Him only through His actions…. Therefore in prayer, when we ask that G-d do this or that, thus speaking of G-d's actions, we speak in first person. And so too in all the blessings, such as the blessings of enjoyment when we acknowledge that He created this fruit or that bread, since we are speaking of His actions we use the first person. (*Aruch Hashulchan, Hilchot Yesodei Hadat v'Hashkamat Haboker* 5:2)

The Torah itself often moves from one person to another in a single verse. For instance, G-d's promise to the Jews in Marah, shortly after they left Egypt:

ויאמר אם שמוע תשמע לקול ה' אלקיך והישר בעיניו תעשה
והאזנת למצותיו ושמרת כל חקיו כל המחלה אשר שמתי במצרים
לא אשים עליך כי אני ה' רפאך: (שמות טו:כו)

And [G-d] said: If you will adhere to the voice of the Lord, your G-d, and do what is upright in His eyes, and listen to His commandments and keep all His statues, all of the diseases that I brought on Egypt I will not bring on you as I am the Lord, your healer. (Shemot 15:26)

As one can plainly see, the verse begins by speaking of G-d in the third person ("the voice of *the Lord*…upright in *His* eyes…"), and ends by using the first person ("all of the diseases that *I* brought on Egypt…"), thereby giving expression to the Jews' ambivalence toward G-d at this point in their journey.

We have seen the tension between G-d's imminence and transcendence played out in Kedusha, in our daily blessings, and in the Torah. Interestingly, the first two blessings of the Amida address this issue, setting the stage for Kedusha. These blessings present G-d in two opposite ways:

ברוך אתה ה', אלוקינו ואלוקי אבותינו...האל הגדול הגיבור והנורא,
אל עליון, גומל חסדים טובים וקונה הכול, וזוכר חסדי אבות ומביא
גואל לבני בניהם למען שמו באהבה, מלך עוזר ומושיע ומגן. ברוך
אתה ה', מגן אברהם. (אבות, הברכה הראשונה של העמידה)

Blessed are You, G-d, our G-d and the G-d of our fathers…the great, mighty, and awesome G-d, exalted G-d, Who bestows bountiful kindness, Who creates all things, Who remembers the piety of the patriarchs, and Who lovingly brings a redeemer to their children's children, for the sake of His name. [He is] a king Who helps, saves, and protects. Blessed are You, G-d, Shield of Avraham. (*Avot*, the first blessing in the Amida)

אתה גיבור לעולם ה', מחייה מתים אתה, רב להושיע. מכלכל
חיים בחסד, מחייה מתים ברחמים רבים, וסומך נופלים ורופא
חולים, ומתיר אסורים, ומקיים אמונתו לישני עפר. מי כמוך בעל
גבורות ומי דומה לך, מלך ממית ומחייה ומצמיח ישועה, ונאמן
אתה להחיות מתים. ברוך אתה ה', מחייה המתים. (גבורות, הברכה
השנייה של העמידה)

You are mighty forever, my Lord. You resurrect the dead; You possess the power to save. He sustains the living with loving kindness, resurrects the dead with great mercy, supports the falling, heals the sick, releases those in bounds, and fulfills His promises to those who sleep in the dust. Who is like You, mighty One! And who can be compared to You, King, Who brings death and restores life, and causes deliverance to spring forth! You are trustworthy to revive the dead. Blessed are You, G-d, Who revives the dead. (*Gevurot*, the second blessing in the Amida)

The distinction between the two is striking. In *avot*, the first blessing, G-d is *our* G-d, sort of "part of the family." He's the G-d of our great-grandfather Avraham, and He is good to us in the memory and merit of our grandparents. G-d is closest to us because of who we come from.[9] And yet, at the same time, G-d is also "the great, mighty, and awesome Gd, exalted Gd."

In *gevurot*, the second blessing, G-d is presented at the outset as a mighty G-d. No mention is made of a familial connection; instead, G-d is so powerful that He can sustain the living, bring death, and restore life. Though this mighty G-d is far greater than us, He uses His strength for us – He sustains the living with loving kindness, supports the falling, and heals the sick.

The first blessing of the Amida focuses on G-d's closeness to us, but it also acknowledges G-d's greatness. The second blessing highlights G-d's might, but includes mention of G-d's loving care to us. In this way, right before we recite the paradoxical lines of Kedusha, we express the tension in the two preceding blessings.

But it's not just in our texts that we find "near" and "far" within close proximity of each other; we see it everywhere we look! Was there a week in your life that was entirely perfect or, on the other hand, an absolute failure?

---

[9] Similarly, when G-d instructs Moshe to tell the Jews, for the first time in hundreds of years, that they will be freed, G-d commands Moshe to say, "So shall you say to the children of Israel: 'The Lord, G-d of your forefathers, the G-d of Avraham, the G-d of Yitzchak, and the G-d of Yaakov, has sent me to you.' This is My name forever, and this is how I should be mentioned in every generation" (Shemot 3:15). Presenting G-d in such a fashion would give the Jews the feeling that they have an "in" and that G-d may actually free them.

Our lives are filled with both; some things work out while others fail. You can get a compliment one minute, and be cursed the next. You can get up in the morning with a smile on your face, but it can be wiped off in a matter of minutes after checking your email.

One short day in the life of a Jew, and one can feel that G-d is both near and yet also far, based on the successes and failures one experiences.

The prayer service mirrors the human condition. Therefore our prayers are said both in the first person as well as the third, expressing the paradox of G-d's glory: He is both everywhere and yet limited to His place. *Davening is not just aspiring for the ideal; it's dealing with the real.*

The tension between experiencing G-d as close or distant parallels the way Judaism conceives of humanity. We are the dust of the earth, and we are made in the image of G-d. We, as the Jewish people, can be demoted to "the sand of the seashore," or elevated to the "stars in the sky." King David eloquently expressed this when he contrasted the human condition in two succinct verses:

מה אנוש כי תזכרנו ובן אדם כי תפקדנו: ותחסרהו מעט מאלקים
וכבוד והדר תעטרהו: (תהלים ח:ה-ו)

What is man, that You are mindful of him? And the human being, that You consider him? Yet You have made him but little lower than the angels, and have crowned him with glory and honor. (Tehillim 8:5–6)

In a similar vein, our sages were aware of both the similarities and the differences between people and angels:

ששה דברים נאמרו בבני אדם, שלשה כמלאכי השרת, שלשה
כבהמה. שלשה כמלאכי השרת: יש להם דעת כמלאכי השרת,
ומהלכין בקומה זקופה כמלאכי השרת, ומספרים בלשון הקדש

כמלאכי השרת. שלשה כבהמה: אוכלין ושותין כבהמה, ופרין ורבין
כבהמה, ומוציאין רעי כבהמה. (חגיגה טז)

Six things are said about the human being; in three of
them humans resemble angels, and in three of them
they resemble animals. Three like angels: they have
wisdom like angels, they walk upright like angels, and
they speak Hebrew like angels. Three like animals:
they eat and drink like animals, they multiply like
animals, and they have biological waste like animals.
(Chagiga 16a)

The very same human being has both angelic and bestial qualities,
and thus this being can be both close and far from G-d.

Summary

When we recite Kedusha, we commit ourselves
to sanctifying G-d's name in the world below as
the angels do above – not only when it seems that
G-d's glory fills the entire universe, but also when
He feels distant from us. Whether it's tough or
easy, when feeling close to or distant from G-d,
Jews promise to sanctify G-d. Moreover, the
prayer service is a reflection of the real, and not
only the ideal; we stand before G-d not just when
things seem perfect, but even when things seem
far from it.

We Pray for Dew? It's That Important?

Prayer is an elevated experience, and we certainly don't want to waste time when we stand before the Master of the Universe.[1] Therefore, it seems strange that in the second blessing of the Amida, we deem it necessary to mention that G-d makes the dew fall![2] It is true that many of G-d's actions are mentioned in this passage, all to fulfill the edict to begin the Amida with praise.[3] While מחיה מתים, "resurrecting the dead," מתיר אסורים, "redeeming those in captivity," and מקיים אמונתו לישני עפר, "fulfilling His divine promises [to us] for all time" are all obviously significant, what is so great about מוריד הטל, ensuring that the dew falls?

We can well understand that in the winter months we petition for rain, saying משיב הרוח ומוריד הגשם, "He Who brings the wind and ensures the rain will fall." Water is the very essence of life, and one can't survive without it.[4] But what's the great importance of dew? Moreover, on the first day of Pesach we devote an entire

---

[1] Berachot 61a states that one should seriously limit the words one says before G-d to avoid paying lip service to G-d or wasting His time, as it were.

[2] *Code of Jewish Law*, OC 114:9. *Morid hatal* is part of all the *nusachim* in Israel, though it is not the common *nusach Ashkenaz* outside of Israel.

[3] See Yerushalmi Berachot 2:4; Berachot 34a.

[4] For example, due to the importance of water, there is a view in the Talmud that before drinking water, one should say the blessing of *borei nefashot*,

prayer to dew, with the *chazan* wearing a white *kittel*. Is dew that vital that we need to devote so much time to it?

In order to understand the importance of dew, it may be helpful to see how it is discussed in Tanach. One instance appears in the words of the prophet Hoshea:

אהיה כטל לישראל יפרח כשושנה ויך שרשיו כלבנון: (הושע יד:ו)

I will be like dew to Israel, he shall blossom like a rose, and he shall cast forth his roots like a cedar of Lebanon. (Hoshea 14:6)

We also find dew mentioned in the words of the prophet Micha:

והיה שארית יעקב בקרב עמים רבים כטל מאת ה׳ כרביבים עלי עשב אשר לא יקוה לאיש ולא ייחל לבני אדם: (מיכה ה:ו)

And the remnant of Yaakov shall be in the midst of many nations, like dew sent by the Lord, like torrents of rain upon vegetation that does not hope for any man and does not wait for people. (Micha 5:6)

It seems from these two sources that dew is connected to the endurance of the Jewish people despite the passage of time, and more importantly, despite the perils and tribulations of exile. Therefore, when speaking about the small "remnant of Yaakov," so small and insignificant "in the midst of many nations," the prophets promise that G-d will ensure the Jewish people's existence just as He ensures that the dew falls each day.

Indeed, there's no logical reason why we should still be around after so many persecutions and exiles, and yet here we are. The code word for ensuring that the Jewish people will survive is dew

---

a blessing usually said after, and not before, partaking of certain foods (Berachot 44a).

– just like the dew will moisten the grass *every day*, so too we will survive, generation after generation.

Since dew relates to the Jewish people's redemption, it makes sense that we mention it in *gevurot*, the second blessing of the Amida speaking of G-d's uncanny and endless might. Just as G-d can do the impossible, by reviving the dead and redeeming those in captivity, so too He will be "like *dew* to Israel" and ensure that the Jewish nation will always walk the face of the earth.

But there is yet another dimension to dew. The prayer for dew that Ashkenazic Jews recite on the first day of Pesach includes the following line:

טַל יַעֲסִיס צוּף הָרִים, טְעֵם בִּמְאוֹדֶךָ מֻבְחָרִים.

Dew will sweeten the nectar of the mountains; give Your chosen ones to taste of Your bounty.

According to the author of this prayer, it seems that dew does not fall to make our crops grow, as does rain, but rather to ensure that the crops will be sweet; dew ensures that the food tastes good in our mouths.

At the end of this very stanza, we seem to jump from delicious food to the survival of the Jewish nation:

חֲנוּנֶיךָ חַלֵּץ מִמַּסְגֵּרִים, זִמְרָה נַנְעִים וְקוֹל נָרִים – בְּטָל.

Release Your merciful ones from their bonds; we will sing a song and raise our voices – with dew.

What does a good-tasting tomato have to do with taking us out of captivity?

Perhaps this is implying that the Jewish people cannot survive by virtue of water alone! *We also need sweetness!* Water represents life and the Torah,[5] both essential to the Jewish people's survival.

---

[5] Taanit 7a.

But it is not enough to survive as a Jew; that life must be filled with dew – sweet, fulfilling, and pleasant.

The great *posek* Rabbi Moshe Feinstein, *z"l*, was known to say that each time a Jew complains about "how difficult it is to be a Jew," another child will have his Jewish commitment destroyed. If it is so difficult, then why bother with it? Instead, Rabbi Feinstein explained, if we care deeply about the future of the Jewish people keeping the Torah, it is important for parents and educators to stress the greatness and beauty of the Torah way of life rather than just the difficulties and commitment needed to adhere to it.[6]

We have to find ways to make the Torah sweet for the Jewish people, to focus not only on the physical survival of our people, but also on making sure that our survival be a story of beauty and sweetness. We dare not speak only about the Jewish people being forced to keep the dictates of the Torah,[7] and the need to surrender to the divine will whether convenient or not. We must also speak of G-d asking the Jewish people if they would be interested in keeping the Torah, and their resounding statement of נעשה ונשמע, "we will do and we will obey."[8] Only in this way will we be able to remove our brothers and sisters from their bonds and ensure that the Torah will survive the passage of time.

---

[6] R. Moshe Feinstein, "Nachala," in conjunction with ArtScroll, 1987, page 45 in the Hebrew edition. The phrase in Yiddish is עס איז שווער צו זיין א ייד. See a similar idea in Rabbi Moshe Feinstein, *Darash Moshe* (ArtScroll Mesorah Publications, 1994), page 57.

[7] Shabbat 88a explains that G-d held Mount Sinai over the Jewish people and proclaimed, "If you accept the Torah, wonderful! But if you do not, you will be buried here" – implying that the Torah was forced upon the Jewish people.

[8] Shemot, chapter 24. See also the Mechilta d'Rabbi Yishmael (ad loc., Mesechta d'Bachodesh 3), which records that G-d did not hold the mountain over the Jewish people in order to force them to accept the Torah, as the Gemara above implies. Rather, just like a dove goes into the holes in the rocks of the desert, G-d held the mountain above the people in order that they would have shade in a very hot desert, thus making them *comfortable and pleasant*!

We therefore find that many Jews have the custom each Saturday night, as they depart from the holiness of Shabbat to the challenges of the week,[9] to recite our patriarch Yitzchak's blessing to Yaakov, which begins with the words **מטל השמים** ויתן לך האלקים, "May G-d bestow upon you *from the dew of heaven*," and only subsequently continues with משמני הארץ ורב דגן ותירש, "and [of] the fatness of the earth and an abundance of grain and wine."[10] A Jew will not be able to survive a week of endless challenges, vicissitudes, and lust for sin without dew – the sense that the pleasant sweetness of Torah is their desired companion.

Thus, when we recite the blessings on the Torah at the start of each day,[11] we ask: והערב נא ה' אלוקינו את דברי תורתך, "May the words of Your Torah be pleasant to us." We pray that this sweetness will produce fruit: ונהיה אנחנו וצאצאינו וצאצאי עמך בית ישראל כולנו יודעי שמך ולומדי תורתך לשמה, "May we, our progeny, and the progeny of the Jewish people all know Your name and learn Your Torah for its sake."

It's therefore no wonder that the psalmist states, עמך נדבת ביום חילך בהדרי קדש מרחם משחר לך טל ילדתך, "Your people will *volunteer* on the day of your host, because of the *beauty of holiness* when you fell from the womb; for you, your youth is like dew."[12] In the words of the Midrash, מה הטל הזה סימן ברכה לעולם, אף אתה סימן ברכה לעולם, "Just like dew is a source of blessing forever, so too you [Avraham and the Jewish people thereafter] will be a source of blessing forever!"[13]

Each time we stand before G-d and mention dew, we praise G-d for ensuring that He will be "like dew to Israel." We trust in G-d's age-old promise: נשבעתי לו שאיני זז טל מבניו לעולם, "I have

[9] *Code of Jewish Law*, OC 295:1; *Mishna Berura* ad loc. 5.
[10] Bereishit 27:28.
[11] Berachot 11a, beginning with the words: ברוך...לעסוק בדברי תורה, "Blessed are You...to be busy with the words of the Torah."
[12] Tehillim 110:3.
[13] Bereishit Rabba 39:8.

promised that I will never remove dew from his [Avraham's] children forever!"[14]

Summary

Just as water is essential to life, Torah is essential to the Jewish people's survival. But in order to endure and perpetuate the Torah's teachings, we also need the Torah to be sweet as the dew. Therefore in this blessing, as we mention all the impossible things that G-d does for us, we also mention that we need dew, the sweetness of Torah.

---

[14] Yerushalmi, Berachot 5:2.

G-d Is Holy – and We Are Too?

אתה קדוש ושמך קדוש וקדושים בכל יום יהללוך סלה. (ברכת
קדושת השם, הברכה השלישית בעמידה)

You are holy, and Your name is holy, and holy ones
will praise You every day, forever. (*Kedushat Hashem*,
the third blessing of the Amida)

The third blessing of the Amida undoubtedly talks about holiness.
G-d is holy, and so is His name. In fact, G-d's name is so holy that
it may not be erased; a piece of paper with G-d's name on it must
be buried.[1] The third phrase, though, is less clear: "The holy ones
will praise Your name every day." Who are the "holy ones"?

Rabbi Jonathan Sacks, in his commentary on the siddur,[2]
explains that the three times the word *holy* is mentioned
corresponds to the three times we recite this word in Kedusha, in
the phrase קדוש קדוש קדוש ה' צבאות מלא כל הארץ כבודו, "Holy, holy,
holy is the Lord of Hosts; the entire universe is full of His glory"
(Yeshayahu 6:3). The Targum Onkelos, the accepted Aramaic
translation on the Prophets,[3] interprets each *holy* in this verse

---

[1] *Code of Jewish Law*, YD 276:9.
[2] *The Koren Siddur (nusach Ashkenaz)* (Jerusalem: Koren Publishers, 2009),
page 115.
[3] See Megilla 3a, Avoda Zara 11a.

as referring to a different realm of G-d's holiness.[4] Similarly, in this blessing the references to holiness correspond to those three realms.

However, I would like to present the perspective of Rav Soloveitchik,[5] inserting a wedge, as I believe the blessing does, between the phrase אתה קדוש ושמך קדוש, "You are holy and Your name is holy" and וקדושים בכל יום יהללוך סלה, "and holy ones will praise You every day, forever." The first two phrases obviously refer to G-d, but the third phrase refers to you and me!

Each day we praise G-d. But we're not just any people praising G-d; we're "holy" people. We, as Jews, were imbued with holiness when we undertook the challenge of receiving the Torah:

ויסעו מרפידים ויבאו מדבר סיני ויחנו במדבר ויחן שם ישראל נגד ההר: ומשה עלה אל האלקים ויקרא אליו ה' מן ההר לאמר כה תאמר לבית יעקב ותגיד לבני ישראל: ...ועתה אם שמוע תשמעו בקלי ושמרתם את בריתי והייתם לי סגלה מכל העמים כי לי כל הארץ: ואתם תהיו לי ממלכת כהנים וגוי קדוש אלה הדברים אשר תדבר אל בני ישראל: ...ויענו כל העם יחדו ויאמרו כל אשר דבר ה' נעשה וישב משה את דברי העם אל ה': (שמות יט:ב-ג, ה-ו, ח)

And they arrived in the desert of Sinai and they encamped in the desert, and Israel encamped there opposite the mountain. Moshe ascended to G-d, and the Lord called to him from the mountain, saying, "So shall you say to the house of Yaakov and tell the sons of Israel.... 'And now, if you obey Me and keep

---

[4] Though this verse is familiar to us from Kedusha, the original source is Yeshayahu 6:3. The Targum translates: וּמְקַבְּלִין דֵּין מִן דֵּין וְאָמְרִין קַדִּישׁ בִּשְׁמֵי מְרוֹמָא עִלָּאָה בֵּית שְׁכִינְתֵּהּ קַדִּישׁ עַל אַרְעָא עוֹבַד גְּבוּרְתֵּהּ קַדִּישׁ לְעָלַם וּלְעָלְמֵי עָלְמַיָּא, "They receive from one another and say, 'Holy in the highest heavens, His divine abode; holy upon earth, the work of His strength; holy forever and for all eternity.'"

[5] "Raayonot al Hatefilla," in Ish Hahalacha Galui v'Nistar (Jerusalem: Elinar Library, 1979), page 261.

My covenant, you shall be to Me a treasure out of all peoples, for the entire earth is Mine. And you shall be to Me a kingdom of princes and *a holy nation*.' These are the words that you shall speak to the children of Israel...." And all the people replied in unison and said, "All that the Lord has spoken we shall do!" And Moshe conveyed the words of the people to the Lord. (Shemot 19:2–3, 5–6, 8)

And thus, once we were prepared to stand up to the challenge, G-d commands us to realize our mission:

וידבר ה' אל משה לאמר: דבר אל כל עדת בני ישראל ואמרת אלהם קדשים תהיו כי קדוש אני ה' אלקיכם: (ויקרא יט:א-ב)

And the Lord spoke to Moshe, saying: "Speak to the entire congregation of the children of Israel, and say to them, 'You shall be holy, for I, the Lord, your G-d, am holy.'" (Vayikra 19:1–2)

Holiness may mean being unique compared to the rest of the world, or it may mean staying away from the prohibitions of the Torah.[6] It can also mean that you sanctify yourself in your so-called mundane life, by making sure that all the permitted aspects of your life are conducted in ways that are spiritually oriented – from saying hello to your coworker, to brushing your teeth, to working out a marriage.[7] Any way you slice it, we are different, since we are supposed to be holy. As holy people, who sanctify everything we do in this world, we come before G-d and proclaim, "You are holy, and Your name is holy, and [we, the Jewish people,] the holy ones will praise Your name every day, forever!" It's not just anyone coming before G-d in petition, as we

---

[6] Rashi, Vayikra 19:2.
[7] Ramban, ibid.

are about to do. Rather, it's the holy people, the people whom G-d has imbued with holiness, ensuring that His name is sanctified in the world, coming before Him with that lofty perspective.

In the words of Rav Soloveitchik (ibid):

> ההלכה לא ציוותה על פרישות גמורה מן החיים או על סיגוף הגוף.
> אדרבה, חפצה היא שהאדם ייהנה מעולמו של הקב"ה. ברם, היא
> תובעת משמעת בזיקת האדם ליצריו ולתאוותיו בכל השטחים
> והכוחות...

> The Halacha never demanded total disconnection from life or self-mortification. On the contrary, it wants man to enjoy the world of G-d. However, it demands discipline between man and his inclinations and lusts in all areas and powers....

If this interpretation is correct, the challenge is upon us: Are we able to genuinely state thrice daily "and we – the *holy people* – will praise you forever"?!

Summary

As a holy people, we have the privilege and responsibility to praise G-d. We try to live our lives in ways that reflect holiness, in order to fulfill our mission of being G-d's holy nation. In this vein we daily state: "We – the holy ones – bless You forever!"

Petitioning G-d: Human Dignity at Its Best

There's often a discrepancy between the original meaning of a word and the meaning that it takes on as it evolves over time.[1] One such example is the term *tefilla*. While we use this term to refer to all our prayers, our sages used the term to refer specifically to one prayer: the Amida.[2]

Taking this assumption to its logical end, one is forced to ask what the crux of *tefilla* is. Glancing through the many blessings of the daily Amida, one can discern three distinct, yet unequal parts: while the first three blessings are praise of G-d, and the final three are thanksgiving to G-d, the main chunk in the middle,

---

[1] For example, לא תעשה כל מלאכה, the verse prohibiting the execution of thirty-nine forbidden acts on Shabbat, has often been translated as "You shall do no work" – suggesting that anything that's not "work" should be allowed and anything that is "work," like carrying a chair up and down the steps of your home, is forbidden. This has unfortunately led many Jews to misunderstand Shabbat in general.

[2] In the phrase סומך גאולה לתפילה, "juxtaposing the blessing of *gaal Yisrael* to *tefilla*" (Berachot 4b), *tefilla* refers to the Amida. Similarly, the Gemara there states that one must first say Shema and thereafter "*tefilla*," again referring to the Amida. For further examples see Berachot 9b and 10b.

constituting thirteen blessings, are requests. We come before G-d and ask for thirteen different things that we are in need of.[3]

Thus, it's no surprise that when our sages dictated that we begin with blessings of praise, and only afterwards put forward our thirteen requests, they use the following terminology:

דרש רבי שמלאי לעולם יסדר אדם שבחו של הקב"ה ואחר כך
יתפלל. (ברכות לב.)

Deduced R. Simlai: One should always bring praise [before G-d] first, and then "pray" [request]. (Berachot 32a)

Based on this, it would seem that the crux of the thrice-daily experience of prayer is but one: *the feeling that I need help!* As one of the paramount sages of the Mishna stated:

רבי שמעון אומר: ...וכשאתה עומד להתפלל, אל תעש תפלתך קבע
אלא **תחנונים לפני המקום**. (אבות דרבי נתן, נוסחא ב פרק ל)

R. Shimon said: ...When you stand up to pray, don't pray by rote; rather, have your prayer be *pleadings before the Almighty*. (Avot d'Rabbi Natan, *nuscha* 2, chapter 30)

You've been there before: you're in a place that you don't know, and you prefer to get further lost rather than ask for directions. It's humiliating to ask for help. It feels terrible to put yourself in a situation in which you look like the famous "*nebach*" who can't do anything to fix the situation himself. Furthermore, in a world in which we are so independent, with the internet allowing us to shop, book travel and more, asking for help is even more

---

[3] See part 4, "Needs: Make It Your Business," for a list of these thirteen requests and their respective themes.

difficult! And the following source may put asking for help in an even worse light. The Talmud states:

דאמר רבי חנינא: ראשונות דומה לעבד שמסדר שבח לפני רבו,
אמצעיות דומה לעבד שמבקש פרס מרבו, אחרונות דומה לעבד
שקבל פרס מרבו ונפטר והולך לו. (ברכות לד.)

As R. Chanina said: In the first [three blessings] he is like a slave who is praising his master, in the middle [blessings] he is like a slave asking for a reward from his master, and in the last [three] he is like a slave who has received that reward from his master and is departing. (Berachot 34a)

I don't want to be a slave – I am the master and I can do it myself! But truth be told, despite everything we can do, we are not totally independent and we still need help. Therefore, we petition G-d for wisdom each day because as intelligent as we may be, we still need divine wisdom to make those critical decisions. We ask G-d for health, knowing that doctors don't have cures for all diseases, and the list naturally goes on.

Though it might feel embarrassing to ask for help, the truth is that the ability to request is one of the greatest gifts that G-d gave to people. We can actually use our mouths to formulate words in order to move ahead, be it to request the services of a personal trainer, to get medicine from a doctor, or to seek advice from a colleague at work. *We have the gift of speech – why not use it?*[4]

The greatest difference between humans and the rest of G-d's creatures is that humans can speak. The highest expression of

---

[4] Indeed, the Targum Onkelos interprets ויהי האדם לנפש חיה, "And the human was a living soul" (Bereishit 2:7) – the Torah's closing description of the creation of man – as meaning that the human became a רוח ממללא, "a *talking* spirit." This implies that speech, the ability to form words, is part of our very essence.

human dignity is that we can use our tongue! With this gift we are able to join forces, together working toward greater achievements.

Pleading with G-d every day in the Amida enables us to overcome the notion that asking for help indicates inferiority. When Chazal liken us to slaves standing before a master, they are teaching us a lesson. If a slave can actually accomplish so much with the help of his mouth – would you not use this tool?

This would explain a sound piece of advice the Talmud gives,[5] which later turned into an obligatory law. The Talmud recommends that we סומך גאולה לתפילה, juxtapose "redemption" to "prayer," i.e., the Amida. This is obligatory in the morning services[6] and recommended during the nighttime services.[7] On a halachic level, this teaches us not to stop for anything between the blessing of *gaal Yisrael*, which follows Shema, and the onset of the Amida.[8] But figuratively, this ruling may be teaching us to combine the redemption of old – i.e., our transition from servitude

---

[5] Berachot 4b says that one who is סומך גאולה לתפילה will be a בן עולם הבא, a resident of the world to come. The Talmud further states that one who does so אינו ניזוק כל היום כולו, will not be harmed the entire day (Berachot 9b). Similarly, one position in the Talmud understands Yeshayahu's affirmation הטוב בעיניך עשיתי, "I have done what was good in Your eyes" (Yeshayahu 39:3) as a reference to the fact that he had juxtaposed redemption to prayer. Here, again, the implication is that juxtaposing redemption to prayer is advisable rather than obligatory, for the prophet would not have mentioned that he has done "extra" good by simply observing the commandments.

[6] *Code of Jewish Law* (OC 111:3) states that this obligation overrides the "worthy cause" (referred to many times above) of reciting one's silent Amida at the same time as the congregation. See the Code (ibid. 66:8), where very precise exceptions are codified, such as one who just received tefillin to don at that moment, or one who has to go on a journey so early in the morning that he is allowed to pray the Amida before the standard time, but is not allowed to recite Shema and its blessings – including this blessing of *gaal Yisrael* (ibid. 89:8).

[7] Ibid. 236:2–3.

[8] Despite this law, the sages established additional blessings between these two prayers during the Maariv service. See Berachot 4b, and Tosfot there, s.v. "*d'amar Rebbi.*"

under Egyptian taskmasters to serving the Master of the Universe – with our daily petitions to G-d.

When changing masters back then, we got a great deal. G-d, unlike a human master, does not require that we clean the floor and polish shoes in order to earn the right to ask for something. G-d wants us to ask Him for our needs as an expression of our relationship with Him.

"איזהו בן העולם הבא? זה הסומך גאולה של ערבית לתפלה של ערבית": יש לאמר וכי מפני שסומך גאולה לתפלה יש לו שכר כל כך שיהיה בן עולם הבא? ואומר מורי הרב שהטעם שזוכה לשכר גדול כזה מפני שהקב"ה כשגאלנו והוציאנו ממצרים היה להיותנו לו לעבדים, שנאמר "כי עבדי הם אשר הוצאתי אותם מארץ מצרים" (ויקרא כה:מב)... וכשהוא מזכיר יציאת מצרים ומתפלל מיד...כן הוא מכיר הטובה והגאולה שגאל אותו הבורא ושהוא עבדו... ועוד אמר מורי, נטריה רחמנא ופרקי, הטעם אחר: מפני שכשמזכיר גאולת מצרים ומתפלל מיד, הוא מראה שבוטח בה' בתפלה, כיון שמבקש ממנו צרכיו, **שמי שאינו בוטח בו לא יבקש ממנו כלום.** (פירוש רבינו יונה, ברכות לד., ב: בדפי הרי"ף)

"Who is a resident of the world to come? One who juxtaposes redemption to prayer": Simply by joining redemption to prayer one receives such an impressive reward? My teacher [Rabbeinu Yona] said that the reason one receives such an impressive reward is because G-d redeemed us and took us out of Egypt *in order for us to be His servants*, as it says, "They are My servants Who I took out of the land of Egypt" (Vayikra 25:42).... And when one mentions the [redemption from] Egypt and then prays immediately thereafter...one acknowledges the good that G-d bestowed upon him by redeeming him, and that he is now G-d's servant.... And my teacher, may G-d guard and protect him, mentioned another reason: when one

prays immediately after mentioning the redemption
from Egypt, he demonstrates through his prayer that
he trusts in G-d – for he is asking for things from G-d,
and *one who doesn't have faith in G-d wouldn't ask
for anything.* (Berachot 34a; the interpretation of the
students of Rabbeinu Yona on the Rif, page 2b)

Both as slaves to our Egyptian taskmasters and as servants of
G-d, we must ask for our needs. But while the Egyptian masters
considered this an annoyance, for G-d it is the essence of our
relationship.

Summary

Three times a day, we stand before G-d "like a
slave before a master," using the very best of
our human abilities to improve our life and the
lives of those around us. It would be the height
of stupidity to have an audience with the Master
and not ask for anything. Instead, the crux of
Jewish prayer is petition. We use speech, one of
our greatest blessings, to request refurbishment
and change.

Blessings of Petition: Bringing Life into Shul

Many years ago, my rebbe, Rav Amital, *z"l*, was partaking of the third Shabbat meal when suddenly there was a blackout. With darkness setting in, and no way to see the words of the Birkat Hamazon (Grace after Meals), the family decided that the rabbi would say the *benching* out loud while the others listened attentively to fulfill their obligation.[1] As they were sitting there in the dark, my rebbe's daughter asked her father if his custom was to say the various petitions at the tip-end of the Grace (starting with the word הרחמן), or to end his Grace at the end of the fourth blessing, with the words לעולם אל יחסרנו, "forever we will not lack."[2] After responding "Who am I to have a *personal* custom,"

---

[1] *Code of Jewish Law*, Rama, OC 195:3. This halachic concept is called שומע כעונה, when one listens to a prayer it is considered as if he said the words himself. See Sukka 38b; *Code of Jewish Law*, OC 25:10; *Mishna Berura*, ad loc. 27.

[2] There is a difference of opinion whether the petitions are part of this final fourth blessing (see the siddur of the Rambam, end of Sefer Ahava, from which one can derive this), or detached from it (Raavya, Berachot 129). However, it seems clear that this is a custom rather than a law (*Yalkut Yosef* 183, footnotes 1 and 7; *Piskei Teshuvot* 16–18, ibid.), and therefore some don't say them at all, while others don't say them on Shabbat and Yom Tov to fulfill the edict of avoiding petition on these days.

Rav Amital answered his grandchildren with an amazing response: "Depends on my mood!"[3]

As we've established, the crux of prayer is petition. By setting petition at the center of the Amida, and by devoting thirteen blessings to it rather than just three for praise and another three for thanksgiving, it seems clear that our sages are declaring that petition is more significant than praise or thanksgiving.

I believe that our sages are teaching us an important lesson: *G-d doesn't want prayer to be detached from life!* Life is full of needs and lackings, of unfinished business and unfulfilled dreams. Our sages wanted us to bring our human suffering and challenges right into shul with us. In the words of the famed Rav A. Y. Kook:

אבל בהפרידו רגשותיו מהשעות שראוי להתרגש ביותר ע"פ התכונה הטבעית של מראה המציאות בהתחלפות הזמנים...הנה תפילתו קבע רק בנפשו לבדו, ודבר אין לה עם כל הרגשת הוד המציאות... (עין איה, ברכות כט:)

But if he separates his feelings from the hour in which he is emotionally struck by the natural environment that changes…his prayer is fixed in his soul only and it has nothing to do with feeling the reality surrounding him. (*Ein Aya*, Berachot 29b)

This idea resonates with regard to prayer on a public fast day, instituted when there is a major drought in Israel:

עמדו בתפלה, מורידין לפני התיבה **זקן ורגיל** ויש לו בנים, וביתו ריקם, כדי שיהא לבו שלם בתפלה. (תענית טו)

They stood to pray; they then placed in front of the prayer table an *elderly and regular man*, who has

---

[3] I heard this story from Rabbi Jonathan Rosenblatt, rabbi of the Riverdale Jewish Center in New York, who was present at the meal.

children, and his home was empty, in order that his
heart be full in prayer. (Taanit 15a)

The Mishna delineates the necessary qualities of the person
leading the prayer service. Rashi explains that a "regular man"
refers to someone who is familiar with the prayer service, such
that he can read the Hebrew clearly to the congregation. This
stipulation makes sense, but the next two clauses are perplexing –
why is it important that the man have children, and why must his
home be "empty," i.e., that he be suffering financially?

Our sages are stressing that prayer is not meant to be detached
from regular life. The opposite is called for: with prayer we bring
our lives into the shul, our needs into the service. Thus, on a fast
day, we need someone who is coming from a place of need, and
who will therefore bring his sense of need into his prayers.

Therefore, it is not surprising that in our daily service we pray
for our most basic needs – health, sustenance, wisdom to make
correct decisions. The prayers in the Tanach are similarly focused
on human needs. The first chapter of I Shmuel records Chana's
famous prayer for a child. After years of infertility, she pours out
her heart to G-d. The Talmud records that this heartfelt prayer had
plenty of spunk:

אמרה חנה לפני הקדוש ברוך הוא: "רבונו של עולם, מכל צבאי
צבאות שבראת בעולמך קשה בעיניך שתתן לי בן אחד?!" (ברכות
לב:)

Said Chana before G-d: "Master of the Universe;
from all of the heavenly hosts that You created in
Your world, it's hard for You to give me one son?!"
(Berachot 32b)

Why is this prayer considered so significant that not only is it
recorded in the Tanach, but it's also the haftara for the first day of
Rosh Hashana, and the very source for all the laws governing our

silent Amida?[4] Once again, G-d does not want only the prayers of those seeking to attain lofty heights when thanking and praising Him; in prayer, we also take our real needs and offer them in request before G-d. This is what Rabbi Shalom Carmy considered the uniqueness of the thought of Rav Soloveitchik,[5] and in my opinion, this is also the uniqueness of Jewish prayer.

More than any other Jewish thinker, Rav Soloveitchik's memorable and sometimes brutal honesty has taught us what both conventional piety and fashionable liberalism often seem intent to conceal: that religion is no escape from conflict, *but the ultimate encounter with reality*. The tendency of conventional religion to edit reality is not limited to the soft-pedaling of existential conflict.

We can now more fully understand the Talmudic teaching quoted above: לעולם יסדר אדם שבחו של מקום ואחר כך **יתפלל**, "One must always first put in order the praise of G-d and only then *pray*!" (Berachot 32a). In Hebrew, the addition of להת (*l'hit*) indicates a reflexive verb, meaning that one does something on one's own, to oneself. For example, להתלבש means that one gets oneself dressed, and להתרחץ means that one washes oneself. In each of these cases, the person is performing the action on him/herself. This is an important clue about one special feature of Jewish prayer. Jewish prayer is a very personal exercise. Therefore, להתפלל (*l'hitpallel*) is a reflexive verb, meaning a reflection...of one's own subjective prayer, a reflection of oneself, at that moment, not of some objective prayer detached from the human condition. Some will have a prayer reflect sadness, some happiness, some a few needs and some many more needs. But no two are alike.

This point is vividly made in the following midrash:

---

[4] Berachot 31a–b. For example, from Chana's prayer we learn that we should say the words in silence and yet move our lips.

[5] "On Eagle's Flight and Snail's Pace," *Tradition* 29, no. 1 (1994): 22.

כבר פירש שלמה "לשמוע אל הרנה ואל התפלה" (מלכים א,
ח:כח): "רנה" – זו קילוסו של הקב"ה, ו-"תפלה" – לצרכיו של
אדם. (דברים רבה ב:א)

Solomon already interpreted "May You listen to the
song and to the prayer" (I Melachim 8:28): "song"
refers to praise of G-d; "prayer" refers to the needs of
man! (Devarim Rabba 2:1)

The need to merge real life with our relationship with G-d is so
ingrained in Judaism that it even influences the physical structure
in which we should try to pray. Regarding the synagogue, the
halacha states:

צריך לפתוח פתחים או חלונות כנגד ירושלים, כדי להתפלל כנגדן,
וטוב שיהיו בבית הכנסת י"ב חלונות. (שולחן ערוך, אורח חיים
צ:ד)

One must have openings or windows that face
Jerusalem in order to pray toward them, and it is best
for the synagogue to have twelve windows.[6] (Code of
Jewish Law, OC 90:4)

While one might think that it would be best to pray in a closed
room, free of distractions, our sages teach us that our spirituality
may not be separate from the rest of our lives.[7] My rebbe, Rav

---

[6] We will address the issue of twelve windows in the next chapter.

[7] Interestingly, the Rashash (Berachot 31a) asks how a prestigious shul in Vilna
during his time didn't have windows, thus violating this law. He answers
that the Talmud says that a בית, a home in which one davens, must have
windows, as codified, versus a shul which does not need to have windows
(as codified in the Pri Megadim, ibid.). Rav Kook, in the introduction to
his commentary on the siddur, explains that while in a home one's prayers
can be very personal and thus egocentric and detached from the world, in a
synagogue this can't be the case as there are so many others around you, and
by default you are attached to reality (Olat Re'iya 1:259). Thus, the need for

Amital, *z"l*, fully integrated this teaching. After viewing the plans for the yeshiva's new building, Rav Amital asked that the architect change his original plans in order to add windows to the main study hall. Despite the extra expense this would incur, he was adamant that the change be made, explaining that he wants his students "to be able to know when *Mashiach* will come by looking outside the windows."

When writing a very difficult, yet necessary[8] eulogy for my rebbe, Rav Amital, *z"l*,[9] I came to the conclusion (as did many others) that hundreds of his students were most attracted not so much to his lectures and teachings, nor to his voice, as to his... brutal honesty, in learning, in teaching, in conveying feelings, and most significantly, in his davening. Seeing Rav Amital leading the prayers for hundreds of students on the High Holidays each year was never the same experience; while the tunes were the same, and the *nusach* precise and unchanging, each year tears would fall at a different place, and joy would be evoked at unexpected moments. Visiting him each year on Sukkot[10] would never find him in the same mood. Thus, fittingly, the song most associated with him is the one we say every Shabbat and Yom Tov in the silent Amida, to the words וטהר לבנו לעבדך באמת, "may You purify our hearts to worship You *in truth*!"

True spirituality is not a few fleeting moments detached from real life. Rather, it's merging life with spirit, and expressing one's

---

windows exists in the private confines of one's home, and not so much in a public synagogue.

[8] See Shabbat 105b, where the Gemara is very critical of those who are "lazy" in not eulogizing a great rabbi.

[9] http://www.haretzion.org/component/content/article/14-home/home/143-hesped-yehoshua-grunstein.

[10] See Rosh Hashana 16b, where the Gemara says that one must visit one's rebbe on the three pilgrimage holidays of the year. Though debatable if this edict applies today, it was something I personally looked forward to and sadly miss!

life's experiences truthfully to G-d. At times it will be thanks for what one has achieved, and at times it will be petition for what one lacks. Life is full of both, and our service before the Almighty must reflect our *true* selves at that moment.

Summary

Our Father in heaven desires our "prayers," not just our praise. When we stand before G-d, we bring our genuine needs and desires to Him. Prayer, like religion, can't be detached from life but must rather be part of it.

Needs: Make It Your Business

A glance at the thirteen blessings of petition, the middle section of the Amida, reveals something extraordinary about "our" needs. The list of blessings is as follows:

1. *Bina,* **wisdom:** asks G-d to grant wisdom and understanding.

2. *Teshuva,* **return or repentance:** asks G-d to help Jews to return to G-d and remove the sins that divide between ourselves and G-d.

3. *Selicha,* **forgiveness:** asks for forgiveness for all sins.

4. *Geula,* **redemption:** asks G-d to rescue His people from their current misfortunes.

5. *Refua,* **healing:** asks G-d to heal the sick.

6. *Birkat hashanim,* **blessing for years:** asks G-d to bless the produce of the earth, bring rain in the winter, and grant us proper livelihoods.

7. *Galuyot,* **ingathering:** asks G-d to allow the ingathering of the Jewish exiles back to the Land of Israel.

8. *Birkat hadin,* **justice:** asks G-d to restore righteous judges as in the days of old.

9. **Birkat haminim, the heretics:** asks G-d to destroy those in heretical sects who slander Jews and who act as informers against Jews.

10. **Tzadikim, righteous ones:** asks G-d to have mercy on all who trust in Him, and requests support for the righteous.

11. **Boneh Yerushalayim, Builder of Jerusalem:** asks G-d to rebuild Jerusalem and to restore the kingdom of David, so that G-d's holy presence will again dwell in Jerusalem.

12. **Birkat David, blessing of David:** asks G-d to bring the Messiah, a descendant of King David.

13. **Tefilla, prayer:** asks G-d to accept our prayers. Additional, miscellaneous requests may be inserted in this blessing.[1]

Let's consider this list: How many of these requests benefit you personally? Interestingly, only about half the blessings relate to personal needs; the others are about the collective needs of the Jewish people. And even within the blessings related to personal needs, not all of them relate to *every* individual *every* day. How many people feel the need to beseech G-d for wisdom three times a day? How many are consciously concerned about the sick on a regular basis? And how many sin so often that they need to be constantly asking for forgiveness? While there may be days when some of these petitions are particularly relevant, *an ordinary day would have you petitioning G-d for things you don't really need!*

So why three times a day? The Mishna may provide the answer:

עשה רצונו כרצונך, כדי שיעשה רצונך כרצונו. (משנה אבות ב:ד)

Make your will like [G-d's] will, so that G-d will make His will like yours. (Mishna Avot 2:4)

---

[1] Avoda Zara 7b: שואל אדם כל צרכיו בשומע תפילה, "One may ask for any of one's needs in the blessing of *Shomeia tefilla*."

Our sages advise us to make our own will like that of G-d, so that G-d will also do what we want. Based on this, it seems that our sages ordained these thirteen blessings because they are what *should be on our agenda* each day, or in the language of the Mishna, they are what G-d, so to speak, is concerned about. The sages knew that we wouldn't necessarily be thinking about these concepts on our own initiative, so they made sure to put them on our agenda.

Hard to do? Of course it is – why would I be thinking about restoring judges when my mortgage is due and I can't pay? Why would I be beseeching G-d for health if my family and I are all young and healthy? Despite the difficulty, our sages wanted us to consider the issues that *should* be important to us. Then, when one issue is important to us personally, G-d will hopefully grant out request.

This is not a magic trick. We Jews are G-d's emissaries on earth;[2] if we don't care about the world's needs, who will?

The alternative, a situation of not asking for anything I don't personally need, is described by the Rambam:

כיון שגלו ישראל בימי נבוכדנצר הרשע נתערבו בפרס ויון ושאר
האומות...ואינם מכירים לדבר יהודית... **ומפני זה כשהיה אחד מהן
מתפלל תקצר לשונו לשאול חפציו או להגיד שבח הקדוש ברוך
הוא בלשון הקדש**... וכיון שראה עזרא ובית דינו כך עמדו ותקנו
להם שמנה עשרה ברכות על הסדר...ואמצעיות יש בהן שאלת כל
הדברים שהן כמו אבות לכל חפצי איש ואיש **ולצרכי הציבור כולן**...
(משנה תורה, הלכות תפילה ונשיאת כפיים א:ד)

Since the Jewish people were exiled in the times of Nevuchadnetzar and they assimilated into Persia, Greece, and other nations...and they didn't know how to speak Hebrew.... And therefore, *when one of them prayed, they didn't have the ability to verbally express their petition or to offer praise to G-d in Hebrew....*

---

[2] See part 4, "*Lemaan Shemo*: Do Me a Favor – for You?"

When Ezra and his court saw this, *they established eighteen blessings in order*...and the middle ones are all petitions, which are like chapter headings *for all the needs of the individual and the community as a whole....* (*Mishneh Torah, Hilchot Tefilla u'Nesiat Kapayim* 1:4)

Perhaps this is the reason why the Code of Jewish law suggests that not only should there be windows in the synagogue,[3] but "it's better that the synagogue have *twelve* windows."[4] There are twelve tribes that make up the Jewish people. Looking out through twelve windows, we will hopefully internalize that the concerns of others should be our concerns, and their needs should be on our minds and in our prayers.

If *we* don't have the needs of the Jewish people and the world firmly on our agenda, how can we expect other nations to consider them?

Summary

We are encouraged to ask G-d for our needs, and even add our own personal prayers. But beyond that, we are required to ask for the needs of the Jewish people and the world at large. *The needs of those beyond our immediate circle should concern us*, to the point that they are on our minds three times a day.

---

[3] See previous chapter, "Blessings of Petition: Bringing Life into Shul."
[4] *Code of Jewish Law*, OC 90:4.

Yerushalayim: Have Patience

Household chores are easier today. Yes, we still have to do laundry, iron, cook, and clean. But with the help of microwaves, washing machines, and dishwashers, housekeeping is easier and faster. Yet patience and long attention spans are still critical for achieving goals, since not everything in life is instantaneous.[1] In that vein, let's glance at this brief blessing of the Amida:[2]

> ולירושלים עירך ברחמים תשוב, ותשכן בתוכה כאשר דברת, ובנה אותה בקרוב בימינו בנין עולם, וכסא דוד מהרה לתוכה תכין. ברוך אתה ה', בונה ירושלים.

And to Jerusalem Your city may You return with mercy, and dwell within it as You said, and rebuild it speedily in our days, and may You soon restore the seat of David to it. Blessed are You, G-d, the Builder of Jerusalem.

---

[1] See part 3, "Fast and Now: Foul Language," for an elaboration on this theme.

[2] The text quoted is the standard Ashkenazic version; other versions have small variations, but are about as descriptive as the text above.

Why does this request include so many specific details, when the other blessings of the Amida are general? This is particularly perplexing in light of Rabbi Meir's comment:

אמר רב הונא אמר רב משום רבי מאיר: לעולם יהיו דבריו של אדם
מועטין לפני הקדוש ברוך הוא. (ברכות סא.)

Said R. Huna in the name of Rav, in the name of R. Meir: One should always say things briefly when standing before G-d. (Berachot 61a)

If all we want is G-d to return to Jerusalem, then we should have just said, "And to Jerusalem Your city may You return with mercy. Blessed are You, G-d, the Builder of Jerusalem." Why add the details:

- "Dwell within it as You said": G-d's holy presence should be felt and seen by all.

- "Rebuild it speedily in our days": the Temple should be rebuilt.

- "May You soon restore the seat of David to it": Jewish government, from a member of the Davidic dynasty, should be reestablished.

It seems that our sages wanted to teach us something, both in regard to Jerusalem in particular, and in regard to Jewish celebration in general: *we don't just celebrate the full redemption; we must acknowledge the small "redemptions" along the way.* Imagine a parent who says to a six-year-old child, bringing home her first successful test paper from grade one: "We'll celebrate once you get your high school diploma, till then there is not much to celebrate"! Just think of a man saying to his bride on their fourth anniversary, "We'll celebrate our fiftieth anniversary, there's no point wasting money until then." Thankfully, most people don't talk that way. Human beings need positive reinforcement for the different small redemptions, for each rung we climb. Without it, there would be no motivation to go any further. We therefore acknowledge the fifth birthday and not just the seventy-fifth, we put on a big smile and give a hug for one good score on a test and not only for the report card, and we celebrate each anniversary that we are fortunate to reach.

Should it be any different with the gifts G-d gives us? There is always room to question our achievements. Perhaps it's not worth celebrating our freedom on Seder night – only six days later the Jews were trapped by the Egyptians at the sea. And even the seventh day of Pesach, when the Jews safely crossed the sea, might not amount to much, as what is Judaism worth without the Torah?! There might be cause to celebrate Shavuot, when the Jews got the Torah, but even then the people sinned with the calf just a few weeks later.

It goes without saying that we don't just celebrate the final redemption, but rather each and every step of the way. As our sages stated, redemption doesn't come overnight, but rather in stages, piece by piece:

רבי חייא רובא ורבי שמעון בן חלפתא הוו מהלכין בהדא בקעת ארבל בקריצתה. ראו אילת השחר שבקע אורה. אמר רבי חיא רובה לרבי שמעון בן חלפת' בר ר': **כך היא גאולתן של ישראל. בתחילה קימעא קימעא, כל שהיא הולכת היא הולכת ומאיר.** (ירושלמי, יומא ג:ב)

R. Chiya Ruba and R. Shimon ben Chalafta were walking in the valley of the Arbel. They saw the morning star beginning to rise. Said R. Chiya to R. Shimon ben Chalafta: "*That's the way the redemption of the Jewish people will transpire; at the beginning very slowly and as time goes on it will get stronger.*" (Yerushalmi, Yuma 3:2)

Our sages teach us to see minute redemptions also within small, seemingly insignificant occurrences. This way, they illustrate that even something as troubling as war should be viewed as the possible harbinger of redemption:

מה ראו לומר גאולה בשביעית? אמר רבא: מתוך שעתידין ליגאל
בשביעית... והאמר מר: בששית - קולות, בשביעית - מלחמות,
במוצאי שביעית בן דוד בא? **מלחמה נמי אתחלתא דגאולה היא.**
(מגילה יז:)

Why is the blessing of redemption the seventh blessing [of the daily Amida]? Said Raba: Because the Jewish people are destined to be redeemed in the seventh year.... But didn't Mar say: In the sixth year there will be "voices," in the seventh year war, and at the end of the seventh year Ben David will come? *War is also the dawning of redemption.* (Megilla 17b)

Even partial redemption is a redemption, and it must be celebrated even though it's not complete. In the words of my revered rebbe, Rav Amital, *z"l*, speaking on Israel's Independence Day when Israel was going through a difficult period:

In any event, we must rejoice today just as we rejoiced in 1948. We must recognize that just as the Holocaust was a gargantuan *chillul Hashem*, so the State of Israel is the greatest *kiddush Hashem*. We have a problem with giving away parts of *Eretz Yisrael, but let us look at what the Holy One has done for us!* We have an independent State, we are a prosperous country, and we are militarily strong. True, there is poverty and there are plenty of other problems, but it is difficult to conceive the magnitude of the change that has been wrought in our condition over the past sixty years.[3]

---

[3] Sermon for Yom Haatzma'ut, 2005: http://www.vbm-torah.org/yyerush/yh65-rya.htm.

By delineating the stages of redemption in the blessing of Jerusalem, our sages may very well have been teaching us that redemption is an evolving process. We have yet to reach a time when the fast of Tisha b'Av will be a thing of the past and we will sit in a glorious Jewish city, permeated with the holy presence of G-d. Indeed, there are stages to the redemption, but thank G-d, we are living in a time when some of those changes are already transpiring:

1. The Kotel, from which G-d's holy presence never left,[4] is in our hands.

2. The Temple Mount, which is still holy[5] despite the fact that it bears the edifice and stronger presence of another religion, is in our hands.

3. A Jewish government rules over Israel, with Jerusalem as its capital.

The blessing of Jerusalem is beginning to come true, and we are obligated to acknowledge even these brief beginnings. But without patience, we can easily overlook these achievements. We can pass them by as relatively insignificant, thereby becoming guilty of not thanking G-d for these amazing steps on the long road to redemption. Therefore, in this blessing we mention *each and every step of the way*.

The Mishna succinctly expresses what our attitude should be:

---

[4] Shemot Rabba 2:2.

[5] See *Mishneh Torah, Hilchot Shemita v'Yovel* 12:15. Due to the higher level of sanctity that still resides on the Temple Mount today, one must immerse in a mikva prior to visiting the Temple Mount and one may not wear leather shoes on the Mount itself.

נכנס לכרך...ונותן הודאה לשעבר וצועק לעתיד לבוא. (ברכות ט:ד)

When one goes into a [dangerous] city…[when he leaves] *he gives thanksgiving for what was and pleads to G-d for the future*. (Berachot 9:4)

Summary

We thank G-d for the good that He has already done for us, and plead for whatever is still lacking. The blessing of Jerusalem in the Amida teaches us to acknowledge the small stages of salvation, even as we pray for the ultimate redemption.

Shomeia Tefilla: Thank G-d, It's Also Maintenance

One late Selichot night,[1] my rebbe Rav Amital, *z"l*, began his pre-Selichot sermon with what seemed like a surprisingly simple question. He related to the opening words of the Selichot: שומע תפילה עדיך כל בשר יבואו, "He Who hears prayer, to You all flesh come." Why, asked Rav Amital, do the Selichot speak of prayer in the singular (שומע תפילה, "He Who hears *prayer*") and not the plural (i.e., שומע תפילות, "He Who hears *prayers*")? It would make more sense to address G-d as שומע תפילות, He Who hears the many prayers of the congregation.[2]

This question is compounded when we consider the wording of the *Shomeia tefilla* blessing in the Amida. We begin the blessing of *Shomeia tefilla* in the plural, stating שמע קולנו, "Hear *our* voices," in keeping with the plural form used throughout of the Amida. And yet we end the blessing by stating ברוך אתה...שומע

---

[1] See *Code of Jewish Law* (OC 581:1), which states that the recitation of Selichot should preferably be said between midnight till a bit before daybreak.

[2] This question gains strength in light of the fact that Selichot should be recited with a congregation. See *Mishneh Torah* (*Hilchot Teshuva* 3:4), which discusses reciting Selichot in shul. See also the *Code of Jewish Law* (OC 581:1), which offers certain leniencies for those who can't leave their homes. More significantly, there are major parts of the Selichot that can only be said in a minyan (*Code of Jewish Law*, OC 565:5).

תפילה, "Blessed are You, G-d, Who hears prayer," in the singular. Why does the blessing move from plural to singular?

Before we answer this question, we need to consider another grammatical issue in the prayers. Before the Shema in the morning and evening, there are a series of blessings that we recite. In the morning we begin with the words, ברוך אתה...יוצר אור ובורא חושך עושה שלום ובורא את הכל, "Blessed are You...Who creates light and darkness, makes peace and creates all." We end with the words ברוך אתה...יוצר המאורות, "Blessed are You...Who creates the sun and moon." Both these phrases are not in the past tense, which would imply that G-d created these things long ago, but rather in the present tense. G-d did not only create the light during the creation of the world – *He is still creating the light.*

It is well known that it's easier to solicit a donation for a new building than for maintaining a pre-existing one – this despite the fact that constructing a new building is usually far more costly. When someone donates to a new building, he feels like he's created something from nothing. Indeed, when he generously donates such a large sum of money to this creation, natural recognition of thanks should dictate that his name should be set in a respectful place on that building. But once the building is built, and someone else has his name on it as the benefactor, who wants to maintain it? It's not as glorious to make sure there is soap in the bathrooms and the kitchen has ample supplies. You can't place your name on the mop and broom. Maintenance is ongoing – it doesn't give you that same sense of accomplishment.

G-d didn't just create the world; *He's an ongoing partner in the maintenance of the world.* He didn't just give the donation for the foundation; he is supporting the daily upkeep of the world. That's why we say in the morning that not only did G-d create the sun, moon, and stars, but He also makes sure that they come up every day. So too in the evening, when we say prior to Shema, ברוך אתה...אשר בדברו מעריב ערבים, "Blessed are You...Who with His word *brings* about the evening," we again use the present tense.

It's not that Hashem created the laws of biology, chemistry, and physics and then left the world alone; rather, G-d is concerned with its well-being, and maintains an ongoing relationship with His creation.

G-d's ongoing maintenance of the world has two consequences. First, we can't fake it in front of G-d; G-d is constantly involved in the world, and therefore you can't "pull the wool" over G-d's eyes. You can theoretically pull one over a fellow human being. But not in front of the One Who knows what's happening.

Second, because G-d is so involved in the world, *He listens to personal requests*. We hope G-d will grant our requests, because G-d knows our personal situations firsthand. Your needs are different from your neighbor's needs, and it's your personal needs that G-d is listening to.

Rav Amital suggested, on that night of Selichot, that G-d hears our *tefillot individually*. He doesn't hear them all together; rather, each prayer is listened to on its own. Therefore we don't end with *Shomeia tefillot* but rather *Shomeia tefilla*, He Who hears *prayer*, in the singular. As the continuous sustainer of all creation, G-d takes a personal interest in each and every one of us.

Summary

G-d knows exactly who you are, and will answer your prayers according to what is best for you. The expectations that G-d has of you are unique to you, without reference to others. Since G-d is constantly involved in the world, He knows our needs and desires and He is continually attending to them. Though G-d may say no, He always listens to each of our prayers and answers in the way that is best for you.

Retzei: Where Do You Put the Comma?

Your Amida is just about over. You opened with the three blessing of praise and then pleaded before G-d for your needs, ending with the generic blessing, "Blessed are You, G-d, Who hears prayer."

With this behind you, you come to the blessing of *avoda*, service, so called because it discusses the Temple service. The blessing is more commonly referred to as *retzei*, after the first word of the paragraph.

This term is a difficult one to translate. It can mean *desire*, or *will*, or favor the Jewish people. It certainly doesn't mean *hear*, since we just asked for G-d to hear our prayers in the previous blessing.

Let's take a closer look:[1]

רצה ה׳ אלקינו בעמך ישראל ובתפלתם והשב את העבודה לדביר ביתך ואשי ישראל ותפלתם באהבה תקבל ברצון ותהי לרצון תמיד עבודת ישראל עמך.

Find favor, the Lord our G-d, in Your people Israel, and in their prayers, and restore the holy service to Your sanctuary, and may You accept the sacrifices of

---

[1] The text quoted follows the Ashkenazic version; other versions have small variations.

the Jewish people and their prayers favorably, with
love, and may the holy service of Your people Israel
always find favor before You.

Looking at this blessing, it's hard to see if it belongs to the former
petitions, or if it's a separate part of the Amida. On the one hand,
we are asking G-d to restore the service of the holy Temple, which
is a type of petition. On the other hand, the request itself is a
communal one (unlike the personal requests for health, sustenance,
etc.) and it begins by speaking in general terms ("Find favor, the
Lord our G-d, in Your people Israel, and in their prayers") without
specifying the subject of the petition, as is the case for the vast
majority of the other blessings.[2] Additionally, while we remove
the thirteen blessings of petition from our service on Shabbat,[3]
this blessing does appear in the Shabbat service. So is it a petition,
or is it not?

The following Gemara may give us some insight:

"לעולם זאת על ישראל" (דברי הימים ב ב:ג): אמר רב גידל אמר
רב: זה מזבח בנוי, ומיכאל שר הגדול עומד ומקריב עליו קרבן.
ורבי יוחנן אמר: אלו תלמידי חכמים העסוקין בהלכות עבודה,
מעלה עליהם הכתוב כאילו נבנה מקדש בימיהם.
אמר ריש לקיש: מאי דכתיב, "זאת התורה לעולה למנחה
ולחטאת ולאשם" (ויקרא ז:לז)? כל העוסק בתורה, כאילו הקריב
עולה מנחה חטאת ואשם.... אמר רבי יצחק: מאי דכתיב, "זאת
תורת החטאת" (ויקרא ו:יח), "וזאת תורת האשם" (שם ז:א)? כל
העוסק בתורת חטאת כאילו הקריב חטאת, וכל העוסק בתורת
אשם כאילו הקריב אשם. (מנחות קי.)

---

[2] The only exception is the blessing of *shema koleinu*, which is a general
request to accept our prayers. And yet, even that blessing talks solely about
the theme of acceptance of prayers.

[3] Yerushalmi Shabbat 15:3; Berachot 21a.

"And this [law] will forever pertain to Israel" (II Chronicles 2:3): R. Gidel said in the name of Rav: This refers to the built altar, on which Michael the great angel is standing and offering a sacrifice.

R. Yochanan said: These are the Torah scholars who study the laws of the sacrifices; Scripture considers it as if they built the Temple in their days.

Says Reish Lakish: What [is the meaning of] the verse "This is the *Torah* for the burnt offering, the meal offering, the sin offering, and the guilt offering" (Vayikra 7:37)? Anyone who studies Torah – it is as if he has sacrificed a burnt offering, a meal offering a sin offering, and a guilt offering. Said R. Yitzchak: What [is the meaning of] the verses "This is the *Torah* of the sin offering" (Vayikra 6:18), "This is the *Torah* of the guilt offering" (ibid. 7:1)? Anyone who studies the laws of the sin offering – it is as if he sacrificed a sin offering, and whoever studies the laws of the guilt offering – it is as if he has sacrificed a guilt offering. (Menachot 110a)

The verse in Chronicles mentions that *zot*, "this" will be *eternal* for the Jewish people, but it doesn't specify what "this" is. In context, the phrase appears at the end of an entire verse discussing the different types of sacrifices, so it would seem that it is the Temple service that is eternal for the Jewish people. However, given that the Temple was destroyed and we are no longer able to offer sacrifices, our sages searched for other meanings to this verse:

1. An angel, Michael, eternally sacrifices on an actual altar.

2. The Jewish people do what they can eternally: they learn Torah, and it is considered as if they brought sacrifices.

3. The Jewish people learn specifically the laws of the sacrifices, and then it will be considered as if they brought those sacrifices.

So according to one explanation, an actual sacrifice is sacrificed, while according to the other explanations, it is the learning of Torah – whether any Torah or specifically the sacrificial laws – that is substituted for actual sacrifices.

Based on these two options, Tosfot brings two opinions as to where the comma should go in the blessing of *retzei*:

> מדרשות חלוקין: יש מי שאומר נשמותיהן של צדיקים, ויש מי
> שאומר כבשים של אש. והיינו דאמרינן בשמונה עשרה בעבודה,
> "ואשי ישראל **ותפלתם** מהרה⁴ באהבה תקבל ברצון". ויש אומרים
> דקאי אדלעיל: "והשב את העבודה לדביר ביתך ואשי ישראל".
> (תוספות, מנחות קי., ד"ה "ומיכאל")

We have two opposing midrashim: Some say that [Michael is offering] the souls of the righteous, and some say [that he is offering] actual sheep of fire. And therefore we say in our Amida, in the blessing of the *avoda* [*retzei*], "And may You speedily accept the sacrifices of the Jewish people and *their prayers* favorably, with love."

And some say that this is referring to what was said before: "And restore the holy service to Your sanctuary, and their sacrifices." (Tosfot, Menachot 110b, s.v. "*u'Michael*")

According to the first option, sacrifices are intrinsically bound up with prayer:[5]

> רצה ה' אלקינו בעמך ישראל ובתפלתם, והשב את העבודה לדביר
> ביתך, **ואשי ישראל ותפלתם** באהבה תקבל ברצון, ותהי לרצון
> תמיד עבודת ישראל עמך.

---

[4] This added word מהרה is found in *nusach Sephard* and not in *nusach Ashkenaz*.

[5] See part 1, "Pouring Our Hearts Out to G-d…Today?" for the opinion in the Talmud that prayer was patterned around the sacrifices of old.

Find favor, the Lord our G-d, in Your people Israel,
and in their prayers, and restore the holy service to
Your sanctuary, *and may You accept the sacrifices of
the Jewish people and their prayers favorably*, with
love, and may the holy service of Your people Israel
always find favor before You.

According to the second opinion, prayer stands apart from
sacrifices:

רצה ה' אלקינו בעמך ישראל ובתפלתם, והשב את העבודה לדביר
ביתך **ואשי ישראל, ותפלתם** באהבה תקבל ברצון, ותהי לרצון
תמיד עבודת ישראל עמך.

Find favor, the Lord our G-d, in Your people Israel,
and in their prayers, and restore the holy service
to Your sanctuary *and the sacrifices of the Jewish
people, and may You accept their prayers* favorably,
with love, and may the holy service of Your people
Israel always find favor before you.

The first option intertwines sacrifices and prayer. Though today
we can't offer sacrifices, in principle every sacrifice had a prayer
connected to it,[6] and we pray that the day will come when we can
again offer our prayers with their respective sacrifices when the
Temple will be restored to full service. In the words of the Rama
in the Code:

---

[6] Taanit 4:2 speaks about the rounds of *maamadot* (rotations) of the Jewish
people who prayed and read the Torah every morning and evening as the
daily sacrifice was being offered. Indeed, the Mishna (ibid.) mentions that it's
uncanny that one's sacrifice is being offered, and the owner of the sacrifice is
not "standing above it" at that moment, either praying or reading the Torah
(Rambam's interpretation, ad loc.).

ונהגו לומר אח"כ "יהי רצון שיבנה בית המקדש" כו', כי התפלה
במקום העבודה ולכן מבקשים על המקדש שנוכל לעשות עבודה
ממש. (שולחן ערוך, אורח חיים קכג:א)

And we have the custom to say after [the Amida],
"May it be G-d's will that the Temple be rebuilt…"
as prayer is in place of the sacrificial worship in the
Temple, and therefore we are requesting that the
Temple be restored so we can do the real worship.
(*Code of Jewish Law*, OC 123:1)

In contrast, the second option separates between sacrifices and
prayer, as if treating them as two separate modes of serving G-d.

So, where do you put the comma? When do you pause when
you pray? Is the prayer part and parcel of the sacrifice, or separate
from it?

It's my belief that the hustle and bustle that occurs at that very
moment of the *chazan*'s public repetition proves the first option:
The *kohanim* move toward the sink, the *leviim* move there as well
to wash the *kohanim*'s hands, and then the *kohanim* make their
way toward the ascended *bima* in the front of the shul. All this
happens quickly, since the *kohanim* are rushing to arrive at the
bima by the time the *chazan* reaches *retzei*.

Why the rush? The Talmud explains:

ואמר ר' יהושע בן לוי: כל כהן שאינו עולה בעבודה – שוב אינו
עולה, שנאמר, "וישא אהרן את ידיו אל העם ויברכם וירד מעשות
החטאת והעולה והשלמים" (ויקרא ט:כב), מה להלן בעבודה, אף
כאן בעבודה. (סוטה לח:)

And said R. Yehoshua ben Levi: Any *kohen* that
didn't ascend [to the elevated *bima* in the front of
the shul] during [the blessing of] *avoda* does not
ascend afterwards, as it says, "And Aharon lifted up
his hands toward the people, and blessed them. And

he descended from offering the sin offering, and the burnt offering, and the peace offerings" (Vayikra 9:22) – just as in this verse the people were blessed during the sacrificial service, so too here. (Sota 38b)

Based on a verse describing Aharon's blessing during the consecration of the Mishkan, the Gemara rules that in order for a *kohen* to bless the people in davening, he must reach the *bima* by the time the *avoda* is occurring, i.e., by the time the sacrifices are being offered. Though the proof text refers to actual Temple worship, the halacha determines that this applies equally to the blessing of *avoda* in the Amida, when we recall the Temple worship and pray for its return:

כשמתחיל שליח ציבור: רצה, כל כהן שבבית הכנסת נעקר ממקומו לעלות לדוכן, ואף אם לא יגיע שם עד שיסיים שליח ציבור רצה, שפיר דמי. אבל אם לא עקר רגליו ברצה, שוב לא יעלה. (שולחן ערוך, אורח חיים קכח:ח)

When the *chazan* begins to recite *retzei*, every *kohen* starts moving in the direction of the elevated *bima*, and even if the *kohen* won't reach the [*bima*] before the *chazan* finishes reciting *retzei*, it's okay. But if he didn't [at least] move his feet during the recital of *retzei*, he does not go up [to the *bima* in order to bless the people]. (*Code of Jewish Law*, OC 128:8)

Why mix the two? What does blessing the congregation have to do with the laws governing the sacrifices?

As I heard many times in the name of Rav Soloveitchik, I believe the answer lies in the interpretation of the term *retzei*. This word seems to come from the word ריצוי, which applies almost exclusively to the world of sacrifices – we ask that our sacrifices find favor in the eyes of G-d, and thus accomplish their respective goals.[7] The word can't mean *accept*, since we just asked for that using the term שומע תפילה, "hear our prayer," in the previous blessing. Moreover, the terminology of the prayer service itself seems to draw a distinction between them. For example, after saying the actual verses and Talmudic passages relating to the sacrifices in the morning, we say:

לכן יהי רצון מלפניך ה' אלוקינו ואלוקי אבותינו שתהיה אמירה זו חשובה **ומקובלת ומרוצה** לפניך כאילו הקרבנו קרבן התמיד במועדו ובמקומו וכהלכתו.

Therefore, may it be Your will, G-d, our G-d and the G-d of our forefathers, that this declaration will be important and *accepted*, and will *find favor* before You, as if we had brought the daily sacrifice in its proper time and place, and in accordance with all its laws.

As one can see, "acceptance" of prayer (מקובלת) is different from "find favor" (מרוצה). If this phrase comes from the world of sacrifices, why is it in our prayer service?

It seems that Jewish law considers the *chazan*'s repetition to be in place of a communal sacrifice.[8] The *Shulchan Aruch Harav* writes:

הוא נעשה שליח לכולם...שפיו כפיהם. (שולחן ערוך הרב, אורח חיים ריג:ו)

---

[7] See Vayikra 1:4. See also Zevachim 6a, which records a debate over whether the term *ritzui* is a synonym for atonement or for having the sacrifice fulfill its mission.

[8] An elaboration of the idea about to be presented can be found in Rav Soloveitchik's *Al Hateshuva*, starting on page 204. Also see part 2, "I'm Part of the Symphony," for a discussion on the Rav's insight that the communal sacrifice (*korban tzibur*) is offered on behalf of the Jewish nation, a single entity that is greater than the total number of individuals that it comprises.

> The [*chazan*] is everyone's messenger...and his mouth
> is their mouth!" (*Shulchan Aruch Harav*, OC 213:6)

The *chazan*'s mouth is like the mouth of the congregation. Just like the *kohen* offers a sacrifice on behalf of the *entire* nation, so too the *chazan* prays on behalf of the *congregation as a whole*. This explains why the halachot regarding the *kohanim*'s behavior when blessing the people today are the same as those governing the *kohanim*'s behavior in the Temple: The *kohanim* must remove their shoes prior to ascending the *bima* to bless the people,[9] just like the Jews did when entering the Temple Mount.[10] The *kohanim* must wash their hands before blessing the people, even if they did so prior to services,[11] just like the *kohanim* did before serving in the Temple.[12] And a *kohen* with a blemish, when the *kohanim* did not cover their hands during the blessing[13] (as done today) is enjoined from blessing the people,[14] just as *kohanim* with blemishes were forbidden from working in the Temple.[15]

It is true that we pray today in a synagogue, which is only a *mikdash me'at*, a "small temple."[16] But these halachot should evoke the feeling that we are standing in the Temple, offering a sacrifice before G-d.[17] Our prayers must go through the very

---

[9] *Code of Jewish Law*, OC 128:5.

[10] See *Mishneh Torah, Hilchot Beit Habechira* 7:2.

[11] *Code of Jewish Law*, OC 128:6.

[12] *Mishneh Torah, Hilchot Biat Hamikdash* 5:1.

[13] Ibid. 5:31.

[14] *Code of Jewish Law*, OC 128:30.

[15] *Mishneh Torah, Hilchot Biat Hamikdash*, chapter 6.

[16] Megilla 29a.

[17] A more radical presentation of this idea is the view of the Yerei'im (404) and the Chayei Adam (17:6) that the biblical command of *mora Mikdash*, to have awe of the Temple, applies to synagogues. Such a view would even forbid removing a stone out of the synagogue's structure since this is forbidden in the Temple (*Sdei Chemed, Maarechet Habayit* 43–44). The Ran, however, disagrees, asserting that the mitzva of *mora Mikdash* as it applies to a shul

same process that a sacrifice goes through! In the words of Rav Soloveitchik:

מזבח יש בשמיים...שלוש פעמים ביום שוטחים אנו את בקשתנו לפני ה', כי ירצה את תפילתנו, כמו את אישינו, כי ירצה את ההקרבה העצמית של ישראל על מזבח זה... התפילה מיוסדת על הרעיון, כי האדם אינו ברשות עצמו אלא הקב"ה תובעו בתביעה שאיננה חלקית כי אם שלמה וכוללת. לעתים חפץ הקב"ה כי האדם יניח את עצמו על גבי המזבח כיצחק בשעתו, יבעיר אש, ויעלה כקרבן עולה. (דברי הגות והערכה, עמ' 271)

There is an altar in the sky.... Three times a day, we bring our request before G-d that G-d will yearn for our prayers, just like [He yearned for] our sacrifices, that He find favor in the self-sacrifice of the Jewish people on this altar.... Prayer is based on the idea that man does not own himself but rather G-d demands of him in a manner that is not partial, but rather complete and all-encompassing. At times, G-d wants man to put himself on the altar like Yitzchak did in his time, light the fire, and come before Him as an elevation offering. (*Divrei Hagut v'Haaracha*, page 271)

Just as improper thoughts while sacrificing can invalidate the sacrifice,[18] so too the *Code of Jewish Law* enjoins us to focus ourselves appropriately before and during prayer.[19] This is not required before shaking a *lulav* or blowing a shofar. Since the mitzva of prayer is like a sacrifice, greater focus is called for. Just

---

is rabbinic (Megilla 8a in the Rif's pagination, s.v. "*v'man*"). The Ramban (quoted by the Ran, ibid.) claims that the contemporary synagogue has the lower status of a *tashmish mitzva*, an object used for a mitzva, just like a *lulav* and shofar.

[18] See *Mishneh Torah*, *Hilchot Pesulei Hamekudashin* 3:7, 12:18, and especially 13:1.

[19] See *Code of Jewish Law*, OC, chapter 93.

like when a person offers a sacrifice, he is meant to feel that the sacrifice is in place of himself, so too when we pray we are meant to feel that we are sacrificing ourselves before G-d.

This sacrifice is, as Rav Soloveitchik pointed out, a complete one; we are not "half Jews," and we dare not have small corners during the day in which we practice our Judaism while the rest of the day is void of our religion. A complete "sacrifice" consists in a Jew stating thrice daily that he or she is totally devoted to being a Jew, be it in shul, at home, while watching TV, while surfing the net, or while working at the office. When standing before G-d in prayer, one is obligated to let one's entire being stand and talk before G-d. In the words, again, of Rav Soloveitchik:

גם כשאנו מקדשים את השם הנכבד והנורא...שולחנו, מיטתו, חנותו, היכלו, הופכים למזבחות שעליהם מקריב האדם את עצמו יום ביומו ומקדש את אישיותו. (רעיונות על התפילה, בתוך "איש ההלכה גלוי ונסתר" [ירושלים: ספריית אלינר, תשל"ט], עמ' 261)

When we sanctify the holy name...one's table, bed, store, abode become altars on which one sacrifices oneself each day, and sanctifies one's personality. ("*Raayonot al Hatefilla*," in *Ish Hahalacha Galui v'Nistar* [Jerusalem: Elinar Library, 1979], page 261)

Therefore, the end of this blessing is not שירצה תפילותינו, "may our prayers find favor," which would parallel the blessing's beginning, רצה ה' אלוקינו בעמך ישראל ובתפלתם, "Find favor, the Lord our G-d, in the Jewish people and their prayers." Instead the blessing ends with ברוך...המחזיר שכינתו לציון, "Blessed...Who returns His holy presence to Zion." As we engage in prayer, imagining ourselves as sacrifices in the Temple, we sacrifice our entire selves to our Jewishness and hope that it will not be long before we can do this via a true altar in Jerusalem.

Summary

The *kohen* conducts himself, during this community sacrifice, just like he did when a sacrifice was brought in the Temple: he joins sacrifice with prayer, asking that the sacrifice find favor before G-d. In our prayers, we too must feel like we're offering a sacrifice, with the same intent and behavior.

Modim and Al Hanisim: Just Expanding the Daily

Throughout Chanuka and Purim, we add the *al hanisim* prayer to the Amida. This prayer acknowledges the tremendous miracles that G-d performed for the Jewish people on Chanuka and Purim, the two holidays that are of rabbinic origin. The other holidays get mentioned during the Amida in the prayer starting with the words *yaaleh v'yavo*. Since *yaaleh v'yavo* is the only other addition to the weekday Amida, it's worthwhile to compare the two prayers.

Yaaleh v'yavo is a general blessing. The content remains largely the same for the different holidays, with the only change being the name of the specific holiday that we are celebrating. In contrast, *al hanisim* is customized to each holiday. After the beginning introductory lines, the main section of *al hanisim* for Purim and Chanukah differs, as the prayer details the miracles specific to each holiday.

The two prayers differ on a halachic level as well. *Yaaleh v'yavo* is recited right after *retzei*, which "asks" G-d, among other things, to return to the Temple and Jerusalem. *Al hanisim*, however, is recited after *modim*, in which we thank G-d for all the miracles and good that He has done for us.[1] And while you don't

---

[1] Shabbat 24a.

have to repeat the Amida if you forget *al hanisim*,[2] you do have to repeat it if you forget *yaaleh v'yavo*.[3]

Rav Hershel Schachter, in the name of Rav Soloveitchik, explained that the difference between the two prayers reflects the difference between Chanuka and Purim versus the other holidays.[4] The holidays mentioned in *yaaleh v'yavo* are all of biblical origin, and as such they enjoy a higher status. These days are essentially different from other days of the year and thus transform a regular weekday into a holiday. The halacha reflects that, establishing what is allowed or forbidden on these days.

Chanuka and Purim, on the other hand, are of rabbinic origin. As such, they are not "special" days, since only G-d has the power to transform a mundane day into a special one. The sages have the power to obligate us in certain actions that day,[5] but they can't forbid particular actions. For this reason, there are no halachic restrictions particular to Chanuka and Purim; any restrictions that are practiced are purely custom.[6]

---

[2] Ibid. The Gemara goes a step further, suggesting that perhaps one need not recite *al hanisim* at all! The decision in favor of saying it seems a bit odd: אמר רבא: ...אינו מזכיר, ואם בא להזכיר מזכיר בהודאה, "Said Raba: ...One need not say it, but if he does say it, it should be said during the thanksgiving section of the Amida [i.e., during the blessing of *modim*]." The Code (OC 682:1) records that you should say *al hanisim*, but if you forget you need not go back to repeat it, and certainly there is no need to repeat the entire Amida.

[3] Shabbat 24a; *Code of Jewish Law*, OC 124:10. However, if you forget to recite *yaaleh v'yavo* on Rosh Chodesh night, you do not need to repeat the Amida.

[4] *Eretz Hatzvi* (Jerusalem: Genesis Jerusalem, 1992), pages 49–50. Quoted as well in other places in the name of the Rav, such as by Rabbi Michal Shurkin, *Harerei Kedem* (Jerusalem, 2000), pages 301–302.

[5] On Chanuka the sages instructed us to light the candles each night, and to recite Hallel in thanksgiving to G-d. On Purim, we have four commandments that we must fulfill: reading the megilla, giving *matanot la'evyonim* (charity), giving *mishloach manot* (food baskets), and eating a meal in celebration of the day.

[6] *Code of Jewish Law*, OC 670:1 and 696:1.

The fundamental differences between the holidays manifest themselves in these two different prayers. Reciting *yaaleh v'yavo* is a fulfillment of the Talmud's edict to mention the uniqueness of the day in our Amida on the unique days of the year.[7] This occurs within the blessing of *avoda*, in the context of asking G-d to restore the Temple, because the day's uniqueness is manifest in the different sacrifices offered in the Temple. In a similar vein, if you forgot to recite *yaaleh v'yavo* you have to repeat the Amida because you have not yet acknowledged the day's unique nature in your prayer.[8]

Al hanisim, on the other hand, is not concerned with mentioning the unique day in our Amida as the day is not inherently unique. The source for saying *al hanisim* is in a different tractate altogether, and its placement and content is different from *yaaleh v'yavo*. *Al hanisim* is a *prolonged thanksgiving* to G-d, for giving us even more to be thankful for on those days. We describe the miracles in detail in order to fully acknowledge G-d's kindness to us. Since *al hanisim* is essentially thanksgiving, we recite *al hanisim* immediately after *modim* – we are extending the daily thanksgiving blessing in words and content. Therefore, we do not need to repeat the Amida if we forget to say *al hanisim*: in any case we recite *modim* in the Amida, so if we fail to say *al hanisim* we have still thanked G-d, albeit not sufficiently given the great miracles of the day.

This analysis leads us to a fundamental understanding of our day-to-day "thanksgiving" prayer of *modim*: we have much to thank G-d for each day! Every day, be it a regular Sunday or mundane Wednesday, we have an obligation to insert "thanksgiving" into our prayers and thus we say:

---

[7] Berachot 40a: כל יום ויום תן לו מעין ברכותיו, "Every day give G-d the unique blessings of that specific day." Rashi explains: בשבת מעין שבת, ביו"ט מעין יו"ט, "On Shabbat [state blessings] regarding Shabbat, and on Yom Tov [state blessings] regarding Yom Tov."

[8] See *Eretz Hatzvi* (ibid., 43–44), where a different explanation is given.

מודים אנחנו לך...ועל ניסך שבכל יום עמנו, ועל נפלאותיך וטובותיך שבכל עת, ערב ובוקר וצהריים.

We thank You, G-d…and for Your miracles that are with us each day,[9] and for Your wonders and goodness that occur all the time, evening, morning, and afternoon.

In our discussion of Mizmor l'Toda,[10] we explained that when something extraordinary happens, we recite the blessing of הגומל לחייבים טובות, "Who bestows good upon the *obligated*," since we are culpable for not noticing the wonders of just getting through a day alive. In line with this reasoning, we *prolong* our thanksgiving on Chanuka and Purim because we are aware of great miracles that occurred on those days, but that thanksgiving flows naturally from our *ongoing obligation* to thank G-d each day for just getting through the day alive.

Given the daily obligation to thank G-d, it goes without saying that if you forget *modim* altogether, you have to repeat the entire Amida. We thank G-d for His kindnesses, even when we don't know what those kindnesses actually were.

---

[9] This may explain the classic question as to why the text of *al hanisim* for Chanuka just speaks about the miracle of the war and restoration of the Temple from defilement, and not a word about the famous miracle of the oil that unnaturally lasted for eight days! Based on the above, this part of the service speaks about G-d's natural miracles and not supernatural ones, ones that are with us and can be felt "each day," and thus only the former two are mentioned and not the supernatural third. See the distinction brought by Rabbi Michal Shurkin in the name of Rav Soloveitchik (*Harerei Kedem*, page 304). Similarly, see *Emek Beracha* (Rabbi Aryeh Pomerantchik, *B'Iinyan Hallel al Hanes*, mainly page 124) where he brings the perspective that while the miracle of the oil was indeed great, the Jewish people at large didn't feel its benefit since it was purely spiritual; in this blessing, we speak about the physical benefits we receive.

[10] See part 3, "Mizmor l'Toda: Thanks for Nothing – That I Know About."

Summary

When offering thanksgiving daily, we are thanking G-d for everything that He has done for us. On Chanuka and Purim, this thanksgiving is merely extended to include the additional miracles that we are aware of.

Take Three Steps Back – Since You Aren't Perfect!

All good things come to an end.

We've stood before G-d, said nineteen blessings of praise, petition, and thanksgiving, and now we have to take our leave. Of course, we make sure to depart respectfully:

> וכשגומר התפלה כורע ופוסע שלש פסיעות לאחוריו...וקבעו שיפטר מן התפלה כמו שנפטרין מלפני המלך. (משנה תורה, הלכות תפילה ונשיאת כפיים ה:י-יא)

> When one finishes to pray, one bows and takes three steps back...and they established that one should depart from prayer in the same matter that one takes leave of a king. (*Mishneh Torah, Hilchot Tefilla u'Nesiat Kapayim* 5:10–11)

The three steps were instituted to ensure that we don't just say bye and move on, but rather that we depart appropriately, being sensitive to what we just went through spiritually. Indeed, this seems to be consistent with previous instances of people taking leave of holiness:

> ולמה ג' פסיעות? אמרו הגאונים: מפני שכשאדם עומד בתפלה עומד במקום קדושה ושכינה למעלה מראשו וכשנפטר מתפלתו

פוסע לאחוריו לצאת למקום חול. ונמצא במדרש שבשעת מתן
תורה נתרחקו ישראל מהר סיני ג' מילין ומשה רבינו נכנס בג'
מחיצות לפני הקב"ה – חשך ענן וערפל – וכשיצא, יצא דרך ג'
מחיצות אלו. וכן הכהן כשכלה העבודה על המזבח להכבש שהיה
בהם גם כן ג' פסיעות. (ערוך השולחן, אורח חיים קכג:א)

Why three steps? The Geonim said that when a person
is standing in prayer, he stands in a place of holiness,
and the holy presence of G-d is above his head, and
when he takes leave from his prayer he walks backward
in order to exit to the realm of the mundane. And we
find in the Midrash that at the time of the giving of the
Torah, the Jewish people distanced themselves three
milin [about 1.8 miles], and Moshe went through the
three partitions before G-d – darkness, cloud, and fog
– and when he departed, he departed by way of these
three. And so too the *kohen*, when he finished the
service on the Altar he descended via the ramp, which
also had three steps. (*Aruch Hashulchan*, OC 123:1)

In accordance with the custom of Moshe and the *kohanim*, we
show our respect for with the Almighty with these three steps.

But what's interesting is the immediate reaction to these three
steps. What's the first thing out of your mouth when you take
leave of G-d in this holy audience?

עֹשֶׂה שָׁלוֹם בִּמְרוֹמָיו, הוּא יַעֲשֶׂה שָׁלוֹם עָלֵינוּ וְעַל כָּל-עַמּוֹ יִשְׂרָאֵל,
וְאִמְרוּ אָמֵן.

He Who makes peace above, may He make peace
upon us and all of His nation Israel, and let us say
amen.

A prayer for peace is always worthwhile; it's been a longtime
vision and hope. Modern-day Israel has been yearning for it

for decades, and it seems to be the agenda in each news brief. Centuries ago, the sages articulated the great value of peace:

אמר רבי שמעון בן חלפתא: לא מצא הקדוש ברוך הוא כלי מחזיק
ברכה לישראל אלא השלום, שנאמר, "ה' עוז לעמו יתן ה' יברך את
עמו בשלום" (תהלים כט:יא). (עוקצין ג:יב)

Said R. Shimon ben Chalafta: G-d found no vessel to hold blessing for the Jewish people other than peace, as it says, "May G-d give strength to His nation; may G-d bless His nation with peace" (Tehillim 29:11). (Uktzin 3:12)

But why the three steps? We say so many words in the prayer service without moving our bodies; why designate the prayer for peace to be accompanied by movement?

This question is compounded by the fact that Kaddish ends with the same petition for peace, and there too three steps are taken[1] – even though we are not exiting an audience with G-d at the end of Kaddish. This indicates that the three steps are intrinsically connected to the prayer for peace, and not necessarily connected to leaving the presence of G-d after the Amida.

I would like to suggest that if you want to be at peace with someone who you feel far from, you have to be willing to "take three steps back," to retreat a bit from your position, in order to come to a mutual understanding of compromise. There are always things for people to disagree about; there are always reasons to feel distant from another person. How can two disparate selves come together in peace? Since I'm right, the other must be off his rocker! He should obviously change to be like me!

The only way two different people can come together is if each person agrees to retreat a bit, if each one "gives in" a bit – if each will take three steps back to give the other room. You may be

---

[1] *Code of Jewish Law*, OC 56:5.

certain that you're right. But in order to form a relationship with the other, you have to be willing to take three steps back.

So states the Talmud:

אמר רבי אלכסנדרי אמר רבי יהושע בן לוי: המתפלל צריך שיפסיע שלש פסיעות לאחוריו, **ואחר כך יתן שלום**. (יומא נג:)

Said R. Alexandrei in the name of R. Yehoshua ben Levi: One who prays must take three steps back, *and only then can he state an offering of peace.* (Yoma 53b)

If we want peace in our homes, we must internalize the very way we arrive at peace with the being Who is most different from us – G-d:

כל המעביר על מדותיו מעבירין לו על כל פשעיו, שנאמר, "נשא עון ועבר על פשע" (מיכה ז:יח) – למי נושא עון? למי שעובר על פשע. (ראש השנה יז.)

Whoever lets things "slide" a bit, G-d will also let his sins "slide," as it says, "He allows the sin to slide, and passes over the transgression" (Micha 7:18). For whom does G-d let the "sin slide"? For those who themselves slide over transgressions done to them. (Rosh Hashana 17a)

If we don't give in on anything – making sure the repair man comes back to screw in every last screw, waiting for the last three cents of change, never giving an inch – then G-d will do the same on the day of judgment. We have plenty for which we would be deserving of G-d's wrath rather than His compassion. But if we're willing to bend a little then we will be at "peace" with G-d, and thus also with others.

Each time you take those three steps back, you are making a statement: I may be wonderful, but I'm not perfect. I need to take three steps back to be at peace with others, to allow others into my life, just like G-d, as it were, takes three steps back from my sins.

Summary

Let's take the three steps back, retreat a bit, and hope that peace above will manifest down here as well – peace between husbands and wives, parents and children, and all our relationships.

 Part V

From Daily Davening
to Daily Life

U'Va l'Tzion: no Insurance but We Have an In

Following the climax of the Amida, we enter into the last section of the prayer service, slowly moving out of prayer mode. Within this section we say a prayer starting with the words, ובא לציון גואל, "And to Zion has come a redeemer." Right at the beginning, we repeat a rather grandiose divine statement:

ואני זאת בריתי אותם אמר ה' רוחי אשר עליך ודברי אשר שמתי בפיך לא ימושו מפיך ומפי זרעך ומפי זרע זרעך אמר ה' מעתה ועד עולם: (ישעיהו נט:כא)

"As for Me, this is My covenant with them," said G-d, "My spirit that is upon you, and My words that I have placed in your mouth, will not depart from your mouth, or your children's mouths, or your children's children's mouths," said G-d, "from now to forever." (Yeshayahu 59:21)

This verse assures us that the Torah will continue to prevail throughout the generations. It's an appropriate statement for a Jew at the end of davening; when the challenges of the world outside are already peeking through the window, we reiterate G-d's promise to always look out for us, no matter what.

But the phrasing of this verse makes us wonder. If the prophet had wanted to say that G-d has made a divine promise that His Torah and the Jewish people would continue throughout the generations, he should have said, "My covenant with You and my Torah will continue to prevail forever." Instead, we say, "My spirit that is *upon you*, and My words that I have placed in *your mouth*, will not depart from your mouth...forever." Why the focus on G-d's spirit and our mouths?

It seems that G-d gave us a divine promise...*but we also have to do our part*. There is a duality to this contract.[1] G-d's spirit "is upon us" to use appropriately; G-d's words are "in our mouths" so we can express G-d's greatness. *We have a gift*. Even before we accomplish anything on our own, we have Torah in our mouths, and the potential to educate the next generation.[2] *When G-d gives us of His spirit, we have the responsibility to use it properly.*

I often think of my paternal grandfather, Moshe (Morris), *z"l*, when I say this verse. He had just turned thirteen before the onset of the Holocaust. His teenage years were spent in literally "hell on earth," through concentration camps and more (as the number on his arm testified), rather than in learning and developing his religiosity and Judaism in a formal yeshiva. He arrived in the USA after years in DP camps, and somehow "naturally" (or perhaps unnaturally) raised a family of *shomrei Shabbat*! Without the privilege of advanced Torah learning, a sukka was built each year, Kiddush and *zemirot* were sung each Shabbat, and the supermarket he owned was closed before candle-lighting time on the eve of Shabbat. This "spirit" upon us, in "our mouths" and souls allowed a simple Jew to go against all odds and succeed.

---

[1] For details on this "contract," see part 4, "*Lemaan Shemo*: Do Me a Favor – for You?"

[2] This is true even before one is born, as our sages suggest that an angel teaches the entire Torah to the fetus before it is born (Nidda 30b). Though the Torah is forgotten once the fetus emerges into the world, Rav Soloveitchik suggested many times that some residue remained.

But this was not served on a silver platter. My grandfather tried tirelessly to both make a successful living as well as a successful life. Never in the Torah does G-d offer a blanket promise. It is always a duality of G-d and humanity, G-d and the Jewish people, doing their mutual jobs. This started right from the beginning. Avraham, the first Jew, appears on to the historic scene when he is told by G-d to move to Israel. However, it is only *after* he actually gets there and walks around the country does G-d promise to give him the land.[3] It seems that we have to do our part to actualize this G-d-given gift *before* G-d does His part.

Even before Avraham came on the scene, the righteous Noach exits the ark, after being cooped up in it for the entire duration of the flood, and sees a desolate world. First, Noach builds an altar, and only then does G-d declare that He will never again destroy the world. Thereafter, G-d commands Noach to be "fruitful and multiple," and only following that command do we read about the contract with the rainbow, in which G-d informs Noach of His decision never to destroy the world.[4] Once again, we see that G-d expects people to do their part, and then He will do His part.

Living up to our responsibilities isn't easy. My rebbe, Rav Amital, *z"l*, would say every year that there are no "*patentim*," no easy fixes, when it comes to *avodat Hashem*, the service of G-d. And in all areas of life, enduring success is achieved through hard work. You can cheat on an exam, but that won't help you when it comes time to put your learning to use on the job.

There will always be an easier way, but it won't endure. Not with raising children, not with building a loving, Torah-filled home, and not with maintaining a happy marriage. Success is due to the willingness to invest hard work, perseverance, and…to the divine help that was promised to us.

---

[3] Bereishit, chapter 12.
[4] Ibid., chapters 8–9.

When saying u'Va l'Tzion, we are either preparing to leave davening in the morning, or leave the Shabbat or holiday with the Mincha service. Our heads are already starting to fill with the daily work-related stress following the small hiatus of the night, Shabbat, or holiday. At that very moment, a Jew has to know one message: there are no short cuts, since hard work surely lies ahead, but one who tries has an "in." Perhaps this is the reason Jewish law dictates that one should try not to remove one's tefillin, worn today primarily for the Shacharit service,[5] till after saying u'Va l'Tzion.[6] As mentioned above,[7] since tefillin is the symbol of G-d's unique contract with the Jewish people, one should say these words of u'Va l'Tzion with it on, feeling the impetus to work hard to elevate oneself and the world with the special gift a Jew possesses. But we have *"protektziya,"* we have an in, so to speak, to put in the effort and hopefully succeed. Therefore, on very gloomy days such as Tisha b'Av we omit this part of the u'Va l'Tzion prayer.[8] On Tisha b'Av we're in mourning and we thus don't feel the motivation to put in the effort when acutely concentrating on all the failures of the Jewish people.

Thus, u'Va l'Tzion is filled with verses promising G-d's support, such as ה' הושיע, המלך יעננו ביום קראנו, "G-d will answer us on the day we call to Him." He will answer us because we have His spirit upon us and "in our mouth"…if we try.

---

[5] This practice is far from simple, but beyond the scope of this work.

[6] *Code of Jewish Law*, OC 25:13, though various interpretations on the Code place it further in the service for various reasons.

[7] See part 3, "The Global and the Particular: Reciting Shema with Its Blessings."

[8] *Code of Jewish Law*, OC, chapter 539.

Summary

As you are about to take your leave of davening, you must recall and reiterate that you have to work and only then will G-d do His part. Don't rely on any shortcuts, be it the Jewish school to educate your children, or any other fast way to deal with life. But know that G-d put His contract *"in your mouth,"* with G-d's *"spirit upon you"* so that you hopefully succeed.

The Simple u'Va l'Tzion That Saves the World

We mentioned above that u'Va l'Tzion is said every day of the year. Thus, it comes as no surprise that our sages refer to the Kedusha of u'Va l'Tzion as Kedusha d'Sidra, the "Consistent Kedusha." But why is that Kedusha so significant that it warrants being said every day? The Talmud's answer is as startling as it is cryptic:

אמר רבא: בכל יום ויום מרובה קללתו משל חבירו...ואלא עלמא
אמאי קא מקיים? אקדושה דסידרא, ואיהא שמיה רבא דאגדתא.
(סוטה מט)

Said Rava: Each day is more cursed than the one before it...so how does the world continue to exist? By [saying] the Kedusha d'Sidra and the *yehei shemei rabba* recited after learning Torah. (Sota 49a)

Wow! One prayer saves the entire world? It's that special? In the regular Kedusha that follows the Amida, we say the same verses proclaiming G-d's holiness – קדוש, קדוש, קדוש ה' צבאות, מלא כל הארץ כבודו, and ברוך כבוד ה' ממקומו. The only difference between them is that in u'Va l'Tzion we add the Targum, the Aramaic translation. Why does that make this prayer so important?

Explains Rashi:

אקדושה דסידרא: סדר קדושה, שלא תקנוה אלא **שיהו כל ישראל**
עוסקין בתורה בכל יום דבר מועט, שאומר קריאתו ותרגומו והן
כעוסקין בתורה. וכיון שנוהג בכל ישראל, בתלמידים ובעמי הארץ,
ויש כאן שתים קדושת השם ותלמוד התורה, חביב הוא. (רש"י,
סוטה מט.).

By [saying] the Kedusha d'Sidra: [Reciting] the
Kedusha was only ordained in order that *all of the
Jewish people would learn a bit of Torah each day*,
for saying it along with its Aramaic translation is
comparable to learning Torah. And since all of Israel,
scholars and ignorant Jews alike, have the custom to
say it, and it mentions both the sanctity of G-d and the
learning of Torah, it is cherished. (Rashi, Sota 49a)

The Talmud's statement, together with Rashi's interpretation,
teaches us two fundamental truths about Torah learning. The first
is that *learning Torah saves the world*. As our sages put it:

והאמר רבי אלעזר: אילמלא תורה לא נתקיימו שמים וארץ,
שנאמר, "אם לא בריתי יומם ולילה חקות שמים וארץ לא שמתי"
(ירמיהו לג:כה). (פסחים סט:)

Said R. Elazar: If not for the [learning of] Torah, the
heavens and earth would not have been sustained, as
it says, "If not for My covenant morning and night, I
would not have established the laws of the heavens
and earth" (Yirmiyahu 33:25). (Pesachim 69b)

There are many things essential to human survival – an ethical
government, a judicial system, police, medical care. How were
the sages audacious enough to put the pursuit of Torah on the
same level as these crucial elements of life?

Rav Amital, *z"l*, often commented that most of our body parts have times when they are not working. When we are sitting, we don't use our feet; when we are neither speaking nor eating we give our mouths a rest. There's only one part of our body that is always working unless we're asleep – *our minds!* Never do we stop thinking unless we're sleeping or dead.

It just can't be, said Rav Amital, that the one part of our body that is always working would go through a day without thinking about the fundamentals of Judaism, the content of our religion, i.e., the Torah! And yet, unless we consciously choose to think about Torah, we could easily go days without considering it. To prevent this, our sages included Torah learning within the daily prayer service. And now we can understand how the world continues to survive – since there are Jews who superficially but willingly devote their minds every day to the pursuit of G-d's Torah by the daily recitation of Kedusha d'Sidra.

The fact that the Jewish people study Torah each day means that there are holy people whose minds are occupied with divine thoughts. The human race is not only "dust from the earth," filled with animalistic desires; we possess divine traits as well. The world may be cursed, but there is a blessed people who bless the world each day with the pleasant fragrance of Torah.[1] If a human being can focus his mind on thinking Torah thoughts, we have reached such a climax that the cursed world should not be destroyed.

The second truth that the Talmud's statement highlights is that *simple Torah learning is praiseworthy as well.* In explaining the importance of u'Va l'Tzion, Rashi states that "since all of Israel, scholars *and ignorant Jews* alike, have the custom to say it, and it mentions both the sanctity of G-d and the learning of Torah, it is

---

[1] See Shabbat 88b, where the Talmud suggests that each time G-d said one of the Ten Commandments atop Mount Sinai, the world was filled with a "pleasant fragrance."

cherished." In other words, the fact that all Jews, be they scholars or simpletons, utter a bit of Torah each day, is "cherished."

We have a terrible tendency to only honor the higher echelons of society – the Talmudic scholars, the wealthy, and the leaders. While they certainly deserve respect, and at times it's even obligatory to honor them,[2] are they the end of the list? What about treating every man and woman with respect? Do our sages not state חביב אדם שנברא בצלם, "The human being is beloved, for he was created in His image"?[3] Is this divine image not worthy of respect?

Where is the respect for those who wake up at five every morning and learn *daf yomi*, a full daily page of Talmud? Yes, they may forget it a day later. But is there no value in consistent learning, in accordance with the halachic dictate to "set aside time each day to learn Torah"?[4]

Once my maternal grandmother passed away, my grandfather Shlomo, *z"l*, would often spend Shabbat and holidays in my parents' home. During these visits, he would frequently ask me to bring him a Gemara. When I would ask him which tractate he wanted, his answer was always the same: "Whatever you bring." His response perplexed me. As a yeshiva student, I spent an entire year studying a specific tractate, delving into its intricacies; how could someone be content with whatever came to hand?

My grandfather's answer was as predictable as my question: "We have to learn, what difference does it make what we learn!" He wasn't a Talmudic scholar; he was a simple Jew, attempting to learn Torah each day. His purpose was not to recall all that he learned, nor to write a scholarly article; rather, it was "just to learn!"

---

[2] *Mishneh Torah, Hilchot Talmud Torah*, chapter 5.

[3] Mishna Avot 3:14.

[4] *Code of Jewish Law*, YD 246:1.

This is the essence of our daily recitation of u'Va l'Tzion. Whether you are a scholar or a simple Jew, we all learn and say the same passage every single day, rain or shine. The daily recitation should highlight the value of the many "simple Jews" out there, who set aside time each day to learn Torah despite the demands on their schedules and energies. They are simple, they are many, and they are "saving the world" with their small acts each day.

If we take this a step further, it's precisely the small, simple actions that are often responsible for great change. A classic example is the story of Rut, who eventually became the paradigm of converts through the generations, and even more so, the אמה של מלכות, the mother of the kingship of Israel, with David being one of her great-grandchildren,[5] and the Messiah destined to ultimately come from this family as well.[6]

When does Rut's bitter tale begin to turn around? Coming to Israel with her mother-in-law as a widowed convert from the evil nation of Moav, Rut had no chance of a livelihood, let alone of remarrying. Her fate changed drastically…when Boaz offered her something to eat:[7]

ולנעמי מודע לאישה איש גבור חיל ממשפחת אלימלך ושמו בעז: ותאמר רות המואביה אל נעמי אלכה נא השדה ואלקטה בשבלים אחר אשר אמצא חן בעיניו: …ויאמר בעז אל רות הלוא שמעת בתי אל תלכי ללקט בשדה אחר וגם לא תעבורי מזה וכה תדבקין עם נערתי: עיניך בשדה אשר יקצרון והלכת אחריהן הלוא צויתי את הנערים לבלתי נגעך וצמת והלכת אל הכלים ושתית מאשר ישאבון הנערים: ותפל על פניה ותשתחו ארצה ותאמר אליו מדוע מצאתי חן בעיניך להכירני ואנכי נכריה: ויען בעז ויאמר לה הגד הגד לי כל אשר עשית את חמותך אחרי מות אישך ותעזבי אביך ואמך וארץ מולדתך ותלכי אל עם אשר לא ידעת תמול שלשום: ישלם

---

[5] See the genealogy at the very end of the book of Ruth.

[6] Sukka 42a; Midrash Bereishit Rabba 97.

[7] Rut, chapter 2.

ה' פעלך ותהי משכרתך שלמה מעם ה' אלקי ישראל אשר באת
לחסות תחת כנפיו: ...ויאמר לה בעז לעת האכל גשי הלם ואכלת
מן הלחם וטבלת פתך בחמץ ותשב מצד הקוצרים ויצבט לה קלי
ותאכל ותשבע ותתר: (רות, פרק ב)

Now Naomi had a kinsman of her husband, a mighty man of valor, of the family of Elimelech, and his name was Boaz. And Rut the Moabite said to Naomi, "I will go now to the field, and I will glean among the ears of grain, after someone whom I will please." ...And Boaz said to Rut, "Have you not heard, my daughter? Do not go to glean in another field, neither shall you go away from here, and here you shall stay with my maidens. Your eyes shall be on the field that they reap, and you shall follow them; have I not ordered the youths not to touch you? And when you are thirsty, you may go to the vessels and drink from that which the youths draw." And she fell on her face and prostrated herself to the ground, and she said to him, "Why have I pleased you that you should acknowledge me, seeing that I am a foreigner?" And Boaz replied and said to her, "It has been told to me all that you did for your mother-in-law after your husband's death, and you left your father and your mother and your native land, and you went to a people that you did not know before. May the Lord reward your deeds, and may your reward be full from the Lord, G-d of Israel, under Whose wings you have come to take shelter." ...And Boaz said to her at mealtime, "Come here and partake of the bread, and dip your morsel in the vinegar." So she sat down beside the reapers, and he handed her parched grain, and she ate all she wanted and had some left over. (Rut, chapter 2)

Yes, Rut set the stage when she accompanied her mother-in-law Naomi back to Israel, following the deaths of Naomi's husband and two sons in the fields of Moav. But the turning point of the story – the switch from death and poverty to happiness and stability – revolves around Boaz's simple, kind offer to "have something to eat."

Is it any surprise that this same man is responsible for generations of Jews exclaiming "*Baruch Hashem*" (thank G-d), almost automatically when they are asked "how are you"? As the Talmud states:[8]

> והתקינו שיהא אדם שואל את שלום חברו **בשם**, שנאמר, "והנה
> בעז בא מבית לחם ויאמר לקוצרים ה' עמכם ויאמרו לו יברכך ה'"
> (רות ב:ד). (ברכות נד.)

> And the rabbis instituted that one asks how one's friend is doing *with G-d's name*, as it says, "And Boaz was coming from Beit Lechem, and he said to those cutting the wheat, 'May G-d be with you,' and they responded, 'G-d bless you'" (Rut 2:4). (Berachot 54a)

One man just offered natural salutations by evoking G-d's name and it became the custom ever since for any self-respecting Jew to use G-d's name when asked "how are you"!

We are about to leave the synagogue, back to the hustle and bustle of life. We may think, in error, that we can't truly contribute to society, fixing its many flaws and developing it further, as we are neither a leader nor wealthy. Comes u'Va l'Tzion and proclaims: You can change the world! It's not just money and power that does it; small, seemingly insignificant acts can achieve change as well.

---

[8] Berachot 54a.

Summary

The Talmud's statement about the importance of u'Va l'Tzion, combined with Rashi's comment, teaches us two fundamental truths about our lives as Jews. First, u'Va l'Tzion functions as a daily dose of Torah that saves the world by ensuring that Jews focus on holiness for at least a bit of every day. Second, simple acts change the world, and simple Jews save the world each day just by learning Torah and doing small acts of kindness. Let's not forget those simple actions and the people behind them, as we head out of our prayer service. It's not just about the big leaders who direct the world; it's also about the small ones who keep it going.

Aleinu: The End or Just the Beginning?

One of the most well-known prayers is Aleinu. And that's not just because we are taught to sing it in elementary school; Aleinu actually enjoys a similar status to Shema in Jewish law. Regarding Shema, the Halacha states:

קרא קריאת שמע ונכנס לבית הכנסת ומצא צבור שקורין קריאת שמע, צריך לקרות עמהם פסוק ראשון, שלא יראה כאילו אינו רוצה לקבל עול מלכות שמים עם חביריו. (שולחן עורך, אורח חיים סה:ב)

If someone has already said Shema, and he enters a synagogue and finds the congregation reading Shema, he must say the first verse [of the Shema] with them so it won't look like he doesn't want to accept upon himself the kingship of G-d with the rest of the congregants. (*Code of Jewish Law*, OC 65:2)

And so too, with respect to Aleinu, the Halacha establishes:

והוא הדין שאר דבר שהצבור אומרים כגון תהלה לדוד או עלינו קורא עמהם. (משנה ברורה סה:ט)

And so too regarding the other portions that the congregation is reciting, such as Tehilla l'David [Ashrei] and Aleinu – one says the prayer together with the congregation. (*Mishna Berura* 65:9)

Thus, even if you are all "davened-out" already, you have to say Shema, Ashrei, and Aleinu together with the congregation.

To be realistic, people know Aleinu so well not because of its halachic importance, but because when you say Aleinu you know it's "almost over." Once you hear it, you know that not much time is left between you and the door out of the synagogue. But when we analyze Aleinu's position in the siddur, we see two different perspectives on what Aleinu accomplishes. In a word, *is it the end or just the beginning?*

The Magen Avraham, citing the Ari, considers Aleinu to be a farewell:

מגן אברהם כתב בשם האר"י שיאמרוהו **אחר כל הג' תפלות** וכן
נוהגין במדינתנו. (משנה ברורה קלב:ז-ח)

The Magen Avraham states, in the name of the Ari, that they should say [Aleinu] *after all three services,* and such is the custom in our country. (*Mishna Berura* 132:7–8)

The Bach, on the other hand, views the prayer as an introduction:

הטעם הוא לתקוע בלבבנו **קודם שנפטרים לבתיהם** יחוד מלכות
שמים, ושיתחזק בלבבנו אמונה זו שיעביר הגילולים מן הארץ
והאלילים כרות יכרתון לתקן עולם במלכות ש-די. כי אז גם כי
יש לכל אחד מישראל משא ומתן עם הגויים עובדי עבודה זרה
וגילוליהם ומצליחיים, לא נפנה לבבנו אל האלילים ולא יעלה
במחשבה חס ושלום שום הרהור עבירה. (ב"ח, אורח חיים קלג,
ד"ה "ואומר עלינו")

The reason is to insert into our hearts, *before going to our homes*, the oneness of G-d's kingship, and to strengthen the belief in our hearts that idolatry will be removed from the land and idols will be destroyed, and the kingship of G-d will be established in the world. Then even though Jews see non-Jews conducting business successfully, they will not turn toward those idols and will not even consider, G-d forbid, any thoughts of sin. (Bach, OC 133, s.v. *"v'omer Aleinu"*)

Since the Magen Avraham sees Aleinu as a farewell to the service, it's not vital to say it *after* all the services, but rather toward the end as a summary of the services.[1] The prayer states that we bow only to G-d, while aiming to remove all other so-called gods and evil from the world, and this is the very essence of our daily supplications to G-d. We come thrice a day before G-d, pleading for a better world, and Aleinu beautifully sums up the essence of the prayer service.

The Bach expresses a different perspective: Aleinu functions as the introduction to a Jew's day.[2] Once we leave the bubble of the synagogue, we will encounter non-Jews, and more importantly, non-Jewish practices. It would be easy to assimilate into the dominant culture surrounding us, seeing how they are the majority, rather than the minority, in the world at large. We therefore utter this prayer to strengthen our hope that the day will come when idols will be removed, and G-d and the moral Jewish ethos will prevail. But moreover, it sums up our very *purpose* as Jews. We are not in this world accidentally, but rather on purpose, as we have a mission: to bring the entire world to the vision of

---

[1] Therefore, *nusach Ashkenaz* doesn't insist on saying this prayer at the very end of the services, but rather toward the end, before the Psalm of the Day.

[2] Thus, *nusach Sephard, nusach Sephardi*, and others place Aleinu at the very end of the services, right before one exits the synagogue to confront the world.

Aleinu in which וכל בני בשר יקראו בשמך, "all humans will call out to You," a world in which moral justice will prevail.

It's no wonder why so many Jews talk about *tikun olam*, a term taken from this prayer! Not only is it one of the last prayers, so it sticks in our memories, it's the essence of our mission as Jews as we move out from the synagogue to the world at large. We are united in that we have a mission to fulfill outside the doors of the synagogue, and as we each exit its walls, we will hopefully fulfill our part.

Summary

While we can view Aleinu as the essence of the service summed up into one final prayer, we can also view it as the vital tool that a Jew needs to persevere *as a Jew* in a world full of endless temptations. By reciting Aleinu at the end of the service, we get the necessary motivation to push forward in our Jewish path. As we leave the synagogue to go into the big world, we dedicate ourselves to the One G-d, and to fixing G-d's world to the best of our abilities.

Shir shel Yom: Then or Now?

Jews at prayer find it very challenging to concentrate on the majority of what they're saying. And yet, there is one place where concentration runs high, not necessarily because of the prayer's spiritual significance but rather due to the text: *Shir shel Yom*, the Psalm of the Day. The reason is simple – as opposed to the other parts of the service, the psalm *changes* every day, and if you don't focus, you'll end up saying the wrong one!

So why do we recite *Shir shel Yom*? There are three reasons given for why it is said each day.

The first has to do with remembering Shabbat. The Ramban suggests that the biblical commandment of זכור את יום השבת לקדשו, "Remember the Sabbath day to sanctify it" (Shemot 20:7) does not only mean to "sanctify" Shabbat on the seventh day of each week.[1] Rather, the verse enjoins us to remember Shabbat once a day, every day, just like many other commandments in the Torah that do not have a specified time.[2] In the Ramban's words:

---

[1] The command to "remember the Sabbath day" is fulfilled on Shabbat with Kiddush (Berachot 20b).

[2] The command ולעובדו בכל לבבכם, "And to serve Him with all your heart" (Devarim 11:13), which is understood to refer to prayer, does not specify a particular time (*Mishneh Torah, Hilchot Tefilla u'Nesiat Kapayim* 1:1).

ועל דרך הפשט אמרו (במכילתא כאן) שהיא מצוה **שנזכור תמיד**
בכל יום את השבת שלא נשכחהו ולא יתחלף לנו בשאר הימים.
(רמב״ן, שמות כ:ז)

And the straightforward interpretation is that we should *remember the Sabbath every day*, such that we do not forget it, nor confuse it with the other days. (Ramban, Shemot 20:7)

The opening line of the *Shir shel Yom* begins with the words "Today is the first/second/third day *toward Shabbat*." By mentioning the day of the week, we fulfill the commandment to remember Shabbat each day. Since Shabbat is so fundamental to our faith,[3] we can well understand the need to recall it once a day every day.

The second reason for the *Shir shel Yom* is to recall the way things were when the Temple stood. After mentioning the day of the week, the opening statement ends by remembering the Temple days: "Today is the ___ day toward Shabbat, *on which day the Levites would sing in the Temple*." While the daily burnt offering was being brought, the Levites would stand on the Temple podium and sing these psalms on the different days of the week.[4] The song for each day is recorded in the Mishna, which is itself recited after Ein k'Elokeinu each Shabbat:

The minimal obligation to pray, according to the Rambam, is therefore once a day (*Book of Mitzvot*, positive commandment 5, but see the Ramban ad loc., who disagrees). Similarly, G-d commands the *kohanim* to bless the people without specifying a time (Bamidbar 6:22–27); in principle, this is incumbent on the *kohanim* once a day (Rambam's *Sefer Hamitzvot*, positive commandment no. 26). Why this is not practiced by most Ashkenazic Jews except on the holidays (*Code of Jewish Law*, OC 128:44, Rama ad loc.) is beyond the scope of this work.

[3] See, for example, *Mishneh Torah* (*Hilchot Shabbat* 30:15), which explains that Shabbat serves as testimony that G-d created the world.

[4] *Mishneh Torah, Hilchot Klei Hamikdash* 3:2.

השיר שהיו הלוים אומרים במקדש: ביום הראשון היו אומרים...
בשני היו אומרים... בשלישי היו אומרים... (משנה תמיד ז:ד)

And this was the song that the Levites would sing
in the Temple: On Sunday they would say.... On
Monday they would say.... On Tuesday they would
say.... (Mishna Tamid 7:4)

As we utter these words, it incumbent upon us to remember
what was, and more importantly, what's missing. It's true that
we just stood in solemn prayer, perhaps in a beautiful synagogue
surrounded by wonderful people. *But there is still something
missing from our lives.* With all the blessing in our lives, we don't
yet have the Temple back. We don't have real sacrifices to offer,
and we don't have Levites singing during their elevation on the
Altar. Each day, we leave the prayer service with the feeling that
we're still not there yet.

The final explanation provided for reciting a psalm every day
is to mark each day of the week. Our sages teach us that the psalm
for each day reflects the day's unique essence:

תניא, רבי יהודה אומר משום רבי עקיבא: בראשון מה היו אומרים?
"לה' הארץ ומלואה" (תהלים כד), על שם שקנה והקנה ושליט
בעולמו.
בשני מה היו אומרים? "גדול ה' ומהלל מאד" (תהלים מח), על
שם שחילק מעשיו ומלך עליהן.
בשלישי היו אומרים "אלהים נצב בעדת א-ל" (תהלים פב), על
שם שגילה ארץ בחכמתו והכין תבל לעדתו.
ברביעי היו אומרים "א-ל נקמות ה'" (תהלים צד), על שם
שברא חמה ולבנה, ועתיד ליפרע מעובדיהן.
בחמישי היו אומרים "הרנינו לאלקים עוזנו" (תהלים פא), על
שם שברא עופות ודגים לשבח לשמו.
בששי היו אומרים "ה' מלך גאות לבש" (תהלים צג), על שם
שגמר מלאכתו, ומלך עליהן.

בשביעי היו אומרים "מזמור שיר ליום השבת" (תהלים צב) –
ליום שכולו שבת. (ראש השנה לא)

A tannaitic source states: R. Yehuda said in the same
of R. Akiva: On Sunday what would they say? "The
earth and everything in it belong to G-d" (Tehillim 24),
for on that day He acquired the world [by beginning
to create it] and ruled sovereign over it.

On Monday what would they say? "G-d is great,
and highly praised" (Tehillim 48), for on that day He
divided His creations and ruled over them.

On Tuesday they would say, "Nature resides in the
company of G-d" (Tehillim 82), for on that day in His
wisdom He revealed the [dry] land, and prepared the
world for His people.

On Wednesday they would say, "The Lord is a G-d
of revenge" (Tehillim 94), for on that day He created
the sun and the moon, and He will ultimately take
revenge on those who worship them.

On Thursday they would say, "Let us praise G-d,
our savior" (Tehillim 81), for on that day He created
fowl and fish to praise His name.

On Friday they would say, "G-d rules in greatness"
(Tehillim 93), for on that day He finished His work,
and ruled over [His creations].

On Saturday they would say, "A psalm, a song to
the Sabbath day," hoping for [the messianic times,] a
day that will be entirely Shabbat. (Rosh Hashana 31a)

According to this Gemara, the psalm for each day commemorates
the events that occurred on that day during the initial six days of
creation, and the way in which G-d's strength manifested itself on
each of those days.

And yet, what was – was! Why must we remember it each week? It seems that while creation occurred in the past, in another sense it continues to be with us today:

כך שנו רבותינו: על ג' דברים הזכיר הקב"ה שמו עליהם, ואף על פי שהן לרעה... "והייתם כאלקים יודעי טוב ורע" – תהיו כמותו: מה הוא **בורא עולמות** אף אתם תבראו עולמות כמוהו. (תנחומא, תזריע ט)

So said our sages: G-d mentioned His name in three instances, even though they were in reference to evil.... "And you shall be like G-d, knowing good and evil" – you shall be like G-d: just like G-d *creates worlds*, so will you create worlds. (Tanchuma, Tazria 9)

The temptation to be "like G-d" was indeed a dangerous one; it was the incentive that the serpent used to seduce Chava into eating from the Tree of Knowledge. If Adam and Chava could be like G-d, perhaps they too would have the power to create worlds.

And yet, we find that we do have the power to continue creation, albeit not the way the serpent foresaw:

מאי דכתיב, "אחרי ה' אלקיכם תלכו" (דברים יג:ה)? וכי אפשר לו לאדם להלך אחר שכינה? ...אלא להלך אחר מדותיו של הקב"ה. מה הוא מלביש ערומים, דכתיב, "ויעש ה' אלקים לאדם ולאשתו כתנות עור וילבישם" (בראשית ג:כא), אף אתה הלבש ערומים. הקב"ה ביקר חולים, דכתיב, "וירא אליו ה' באלוני ממרא" (שם יח:א), אף אתה בקר חולים. הקב"ה ניחם אבלים, דכתיב, "ויהי אחרי מות אברהם ויברך אלקים את יצחק בנו" (שם כה:יא), אף אתה נחם אבלים. (סוטה יד.)

What does it mean when it says, "After the Lord your G-d you shall follow" (Devarim 13:5)? Is it possible for a human being to walk after G-d? ...Rather it means to follow in the behavior of G-d. Just like G-d clothes the naked, as it says, "And the Lord G-d made leather clothing for Adam and his wife and He clothed them" (Bereishit 3:21), so too you. Just like G-d visits the sick, as it says, "And G-d appeared to him in Alonei Mamre" (ibid. 18:1), so too you. Just like G-d comforted the bereaved, as it says, "Following the death of Avraham G-d blessed his son Yitzchak" (ibid. 25:11), so too you. (Sota 14a)

We can't create something from nothing, like G-d did during creation, but we can surely perform the acts of kindness that the Torah describes, thereby emulating G-d in our own way. When we recite the daily psalm we recall creation, *in order that we continue to emulate G-d's loving kindness* in continuing to create and develop this world. Creation was not just then, it's with us now, as we continue to create new frontiers for the values of G-d to reign.

Summary

The Psalm of the Day deserves an added level of concentration for three reasons:

1. To remember the Shabbat daily.

2. To recall that life is not yet complete without the Temple.

3. To ensure, as we prepare to exit the synagogue, that we will continue to develop the world in keeping with G-d's first loving, creative act.

Summary of Themes

Part I: A Jew at Prayer

Pouring Our Hearts Out to G-d...Today?

Regulated prayer, thrice daily, at specific times and from a set text of the siddur, has taken the place of heart-filled, spontaneous prayer. However, the sages feared that Jews would go through life experiences daily without connecting them to their religion and G-d. With established prayer, Jews have these *spiritual interruptions* at different intervals throughout the day, ensuring that Jewish core beliefs remain an integral part of our consciousness daily.

Daven – with the Mindset of a Baby

As we face the Holy of Holies three times a day, the place in which two faces of babies adorned the top of the Holy Ark, let us not forget to be in the mindset of children: totally secure, totally dedicated, and totally without grudges!

What Happened to the *Yasher Koach* Culture?

Thank G-d, the "*yasher koach*" culture lives on in the synagogue, where *we simply acknowledge one another's existence*. Let's hope it spreads far beyond the synagogue to the people that we meet throughout our day.

Part II: A Jew at a Minyan

The Quandary of Praying in a Group
Lack of spontaneity, peer pressure, and distractions are built into a typical minyan. However, engaging in the laws of prayer may enable us to use minyan to deepen our own prayer experience, and our relationship to the community at large.

A Group Effort That Helps Me
Since we can't always have intent for the words we say, *the others "cover us" by virtue of their private intent, or by virtue of the* chazan's *repetition of the service.* Through this combined effort, an authentic prayer will hopefully be prayed before G-d.

Praying with a Minyan – for Better and for Worse
A minyan forces a Jew *to connect to the Jewish people*, with all their inevitable problems. Minyan takes us out of our bubbles, and reconnects us to the public thoroughfare of the Jewish people.

Don't Forget the Individual
The shul is for individuals to become inspired and grow. *The individual must have his place* even as we all daven together as part of a bigger whole.

Minyan: The Anti-Egocentric Daily
Acknowledging the other is part and parcel of davening in a minyan. Regular minyan attendance can therefore help us become more considerate and attentive in our relationships to the significant others who are part of our lives.

I'm Part of the Symphony
By neglecting the minyan you are considered a "bad neighbor," *because you are not joining the community's symphony.* Conversely, when you do pray in a minyan, the "symphony" will sound better, and even if your own contribution to the music is

minimal, you will receive the "applause" that the entire symphony will hopefully receive from on high.

Part III: Walking toward the Amida

Birkot Hashachar: Don't Let a *Yud* Become a *Vav*
Birkot Hashachar remind us to acknowledge *all the normal activities that we do every day*. Let's not wait until the good things in our lives disappear; instead, let's appreciate the precious blessings in our lives every day while they are still here.

Mizmor l'Toda: Thanks for Nothing – That I Know About
We thank G-d "for nothing," or at least nothing that we know about. Though we aren't aware of the hidden miracles that G-d does for us daily, *we acknowledge His silent intervention in our lives through these psalms of praise* before we begin the Shema and its blessings.

Ashrei: From A–Z and That's It?
Words alone can do justice in praising G-d properly, but not total justice. We therefore limit ourselves to the acrostic of the alphabet, and that limitation highlights the power and limit of words, *and the feeling that much more should be said to our spouses, our children, our friends, and of course to G-d.*

The Global and the Particular: Reciting Shema with Its Blessings
We recite two blessings in order to prepare ourselves to accept the yoke of heaven with Shema. These blessings teach us that as G-d's children, *we are responsible both for ourselves as well as all of G-d's creations.* We dare not just be a shining example for the former; rather we must also uphold our obligation to the latter.

Fast and Now: Foul Language
Every morning and evening, before accepting the yoke of heaven in Shema, a Jew declares: "Though I live in the fast-and-now generation, I will fight to develop my trait of patience, *to invest the time and effort needed in order to be a devoted soldier in G-d's army.*"

Part IV: The Amida: A Daily Audience with G-d

Hashem Sefatai Tiftach: An Innovative Addition and Nobody Screams "Reformer"?
We begin the Amida by stating, "G-d, please open my lips and let my mouth utter Your praises." *This verse expresses the essence of prayer: the desire to give form to what lies in our hearts.* When the essence of prayer is added, there is no discussion!

"Welcome Back" after the Amida?
Don't jump into the Amida! Take a few seconds, and try to clear your head and create a prayer, rather than a four-minute lip service. Easy it's not, vital it is.

Praise – G-d Needs a Mortal to Praise Him?
We don't praise G-d in order to "butter up" G-d to our request, G-d forbid. Rather, our praise is there to acknowledge the greatness of G-d, so that we understand that despite all our achievements, as great as we may think we are, we don't approach the greatness of G-d. This helps prevent us from taking ourselves too seriously.

Lemaan Shemo: Do Me a Favor – for You?
Do it for us because we represent You. We're in it together. Do it for You! We're partners.

"Near," "No, Far," Say the Two-Headed Monsters: The First Two Blessings of the Amida and Kedusha

We commit ourselves to sanctifying G-d's name *not only when it seems that G-d's glory fills the entire universe, but also when He feels distant from us.* We stand before G-d not just when things seem perfect, but even when things seem far from it. Often enough, both are true at the same time!

We Pray for Dew? It's That Important?

In order to perpetuate the Torah's teachings, we also need the Torah to be sweet as the dew. So in this blessing, in which we mention all the amazing things that G-d does for us, we also mention that we need "dew."

G-d Is Holy – and We Are Too?

As a holy people, we have the privilege and responsibility to praise G-d. We try to live our lives in ways that reflect holiness, in order to fulfill our mission of being G-d's holy nation.

Petitioning G-d: Human Dignity at Its Best

Three times a day, we use the very best of our human abilities to improve our lives. It would be the height of stupidity to have an audience with the Master and not ask for anything. We use speech, one of our greatest blessings, to request refurbishment and change.

Blessings of Petition: Bringing Life into Shul

Our Father in heaven desires "prayers," not just praise. When we stand before G-d, we bring our genuine needs and desires to Him, since prayer, like religion, can't be detached from life.

Needs: Make It Your Business

We are required to ask G-d for our needs, as well as the needs of the Jewish people and the world at large. *The needs of those beyond our immediate circle should concern us*, to the point that they are on our minds three times a day.

Yerushalayim: Have Patience
We thank G-d for the good that He has already done for us, and plead for whatever we still lack. The blessing of Jerusalem in the Amida teaches us to acknowledge the small stages of salvation, the small redemptions, even as we pray for the ultimate redemption.

Shomeia Tefilla: **Thank G-d, It's Also Maintenance**
G-d knows exactly who you are, where you stand in life, and what your needs are. Thus, G-d will answer your prayers according to what is best *for you*. Since G-d is constantly involved in the world, He knows *your* needs and desires. Though G-d may say no, He always listens to each of your prayers.

Retzei: **Where Do You Put the Comma?**
The *kohen* conducts himself, during this community sacrifice, just like he did when a sacrifice was brought in the Temple. In our prayers, we too must feel like we're offering a sacrifice, with the same intent and behavior.

Modim **and** *Al Hanisim*: **Just Expanding the Daily**
We offer thanksgiving daily for everything that G-d has done for us. On Chanuka and Purim, this thanksgiving is merely extended to include the additional miracles that we are aware of.

Take Three Steps Back – Since You Aren't Perfect!
Let's take the three steps back, retreat a bit, and hope that peace above will manifest down here as well.

Part V: From Daily Davening to Daily Life

U'Va l'Tzion: No Insurance but We Have an In
You have to work and only then will G-d do His part. Don't rely on any shortcuts, be it the Jewish school to educate your children, or any other fast way to deal with life. But know that you have an

"in," as G-d put His contract "in your mouth," with G-d's "spirit upon you" so that you hopefully succeed.

The Simple u'Va l'Tzion That Saves the World

U'Va l'Tzion functions as a daily dose of Torah that saves the world by ensuring that Jews focus on holiness for at least a bit of every day. In addition, simple Jews save the world each day just by learning Torah and engaging in good deeds. As we head out of our prayer service, let's not forget those simple actions and the people behind them.

Aleinu: The End or Just the Beginning?

By reciting Aleinu at the end of the service, we get the necessary motivation, summing up all we just said, to push forward in our Jewish path outside the confines of prayer. As we leave the synagogue to go into the big world, we dedicate ourselves to our mission outside the synagogue: to fix the world so all will be under the kingship of G-d.

Shir shel Yom: Then or Now?

The Psalm of the Day deserves an added level of concentration for three reasons: to remember the Shabbat daily, to recall that life is not yet complete without the Temple, and to ensure, as we prepare to exit the synagogue, that we will continue to develop the world in keeping with G-d's initial creative act.